A JOURNEY THROUGH

Inadequacy

Written by Paul G. Otke, Ph.D.

Note for Librarians: a cataloguing record for this book that includes Dewey Classification and US Library of Congress numbers is available from the National Library of Canada. The complete cataloguing record can be obtained from the National Library's online database at: www.nlc-bnc.ca/amicus/index-e.html

ISBN 1-4120-1304-6

TRAFFORD

This book was published _on-demand_ in cooperation with Trafford Publishing. On-demand publishing is a unique process and service of making a book available for retail sale to the public taking advantage of on-demand manufacturing and Internet marketing. **On-demand publishing** includes promotions, retail sales, manufacturing, order fulfilment, accounting and collecting royalties on behalf of the author.

Suite 6E, 2333 Government St., Victoria, B.C. V8T 4P4, CANADA

Phone	250-383-6864	Toll-free	1-888-232-4444 (Canada & US)
Fax	250-383-6804	E-mail	sales@trafford.com
Web site	www.trafford.com	TRAFFORD PUBLISHING IS A DIVISION OF TRAFFORD HOLDINGS LTD.	
Trafford Catalogue #03-1682		www.trafford.com/robots/03-1682.html	

10   9   8   7   6   5   4   3   2

To

My wife Selma, my loving, tolerant and inspirational friend and to my four children, Carmen, Rhoda, Laura and Jayson who have made parenting worthwhile.

This book is especially dedicated to the memory of my parents Lydia and August whose remarkable love gave me, an orphan boy, my start in life.

Acknowledgements

Two people merit special mention: Dr. Jose Bustillo and Mrs. Mary Dawe. Jose, who so generously put his artistic talents to work in the creation of various sketches which greatly enhanced the written word. His sensitive interpretations and humorous presentations so well captured what I could not describe.

Mary is a tenacious task master whose editorial skills are noteworthy. She devoted many hours modifying and refining what I had painstakingly but unskillfully created. Her patient modifications and corrections, sensitively given, resulted in marked improvements while still preserving our friendship.

I also owe a great debt of gratitude to the many people whose encouragement and support provided the incentive needed to put pen to paper. Others, provided design suggestions and undertook tedious proofreading tasks. Scott Cassels also deserves thanks for his book cover design suggestions.

My wife, Selma, deserves special recognition for tolerating my frustrated outbursts while still lovingly encouraging me to continue.

Prelude

At various times in my life, I've reflected on decisions made, successes and failures, high and low points. Such reflections frequently opened doors I preferred to leave closed.

Frequently I meditated on what might have happened had I chosen alternate routes or had not been influenced by certain people along the way. What if I had stayed home that evening rather than attend a function where I met the love of my life.

I remember often feeling very insecure, threatened and second class. At the same time, positive uplifting events balanced the scales for me. Both experiences influenced decision-making. Telling my life's story in biographical form reflects this balance.

Doing so, I emphasize that we all have feelings of insufficiency, even those who appear completely self-assured — but we all have the capacity to rise above such feelings.

Historical reflections are included at the prompting of my children and grandchildren whose fascination with the past justified my wanderings.

> *To feel inadequate is to be human.*
> *Alfred Adler — Psychologist*

Contents

Chapter One
The Historical Past

None of us live in a vacuum; we all have a past that influenced our development. One cannot fully understand the present without an awareness of where we came from — the impact of the formative events that determined how we viewed ourselves and how we reacted to life's events.

Where should such a story begin? How we feel about ourselves, has a long historical base. Knowing a bit about one's history, the beliefs, values and attitudes that helped mould the way we feel, provides a glimpse into the inner self — a clue to the puzzle.

Back to my story — my feelings of inadequacy and how such feelings were shaped and modified, leading eventually to a better acceptance of myself — the real me without all the window dressing! This entails a bit of exploration. One never really escapes one's past. The voice of one's parents never leaves us. We may suppress such voices, push them to the level of unconsciousness, but they will always be there perking away and making their presence felt — speaking and influencing us in subtle ways.

What voices have spoken to me over the years and how have they affected me? Were they positive or negative influences? How did they touch me and cause me to feel inadequate or self-confident? How did they modify my behaviour? Sharing these may provide a better understanding of inadequacy and how to deal with such feelings. This means going back, revealing a bit of my roots at various stages of my life, the experiences which formed me, the associated feelings and resultant behaviours. Doing so, others with feelings of inadequacy may come to realize they are not alone, regardless of their status and time of life. Accepting the reality that we all feel deficient under certain circumstances helps overcome limitations. Coming to terms with such feelings, bringing them out in the open, provides new and helpful insights. Such a broadened awareness helps one to live a fuller life unencumbered by past events that cannot be changed but must be faced to neutralize their grip.

Like so many parents at the turn of the twentieth century, Europe was my parents' place of origin. Poland was their birthplace and early home. Here they received their grounding, which they imparted to their children. Schooling for women was not considered necessary since marriage and home building was viewed as the primary and, in many instances, the only vocation. This being so, my mother Lydia, although very bright, received little formal schooling even though she came from a family where her grandfather and several of his brothers had been school teachers. My father August, in keeping with expectations, completed primary school. Shortly thereafter, he was conscripted into the Russian military where he served in Czar Nicholas II's Security Guard. Being tall in stature undoubtedly enhanced his appearance in uniform. Following his release from the military, romance was in the air stimulated by Lydia's appeal. This must have been considerable, since she previously had been engaged three times prior to marrying August one month short of her seventeenth birthday. With the on-going unrest in the area, survival became the central concern. This led August to depart for Canada in 1910, finally settling in Winnipeg. Here his preoccupation was to earn enough money to have his family join him — a time of loneliness for him and Lydia. A three-year separation left Lydia behind caring for several young children.

Finally, saying good bye to relatives, not to be seen again, Lydia left to join her husband in a strange land. After weeks on a ship, numerous days on a train through barren land, finally the family was reunited. Both parents being strong personalities, a melding of the two in Canada undoubtedly took some adjusting.

Hard times resulted in the loss of their city home and a move to northern Manitoba — homestead country. Here they took up temporary residence in an abandoned log house. Moss inserted in the cracks between the logs, reinforced by wet clay that eventually hardened, kept out the wind and dust. The inside was brightened by sunlight through cracked windows by day and at night a coal oil lamp, sparingly used to save coal oil, dimly lit the inside. The log walls were brightened by calcimine, a white tinted powder mixed with water, and applied by a brush. This created a look of hominess. At least the family was together safe from political unrest. A helpful neighbour, recognizing the plight of the family, lent a cow providing fresh milk for the young children. Hampers of home canned vegetables, fruits, chicken and beef tied the family over until August and an older son earned money as a farm labourer.

Stormy weather is what man needs from time to time
to remind him he's not really in charge of anything!
Author — unknown

In due course, the family earned enough money for a down payment on a quarter section of land nearby. Fortunately, August was a talented carpenter. This and his cabinetmaker skills were quickly put to use building a frame home, one of the few in the district — something which set our family apart. August's ability and ingenuity led to various resourceful undertakings. A cistern (underground reservoir) was built under the summer kitchen to catch the rainwater from the roof. A hand pump carried the water to the kitchen. An icehouse served as a modern day fridge. This consisted of a hand-dug hole under a small building, which was liberally sprinkled with sawdust. Into this large chunks of ice, cut from a near by slough during the winter, were inserted in jigsaw fashion. Additional sawdust spread over the ice served as an insulator. Into this space were placed milk, cream and other foods requiring refrigeration. The ice gradually melted and disappeared into the ground but kept things cool throughout the hot summer. A similar cellar was constructed under the house where potatoes, vegetables, canned goods and, of course, home-made dandelion wine were stored. A pump house, housing a onelunger engine, was eventually built to pump water for domestic and local use. Prior to that, water was manually pumped and animal needs satisfied by water hauled in large barrels from a nearby slough on what was called a, stone Boat, a horse drawn sled.

The Depression failed to weaken the hope for better times soundly rooted in a strong faith. Food, clothing and farming costs consumed available funds. This, however, did not stifle ambition or the belief that hard work and determination would provide a brighter future. While my parents strongly endorsed higher education, money simply was not available to help their children continue their schooling beyond grade eight. Those wishing to continue, earned the funds needed by doing housekeeping duties, part-time jobs, or simply working until sufficient monies were accumulated. Parental conviction generated a farmer, a storekeeper, two nurses, a school teacher, a medical doctor, a pastor, and a psychologist, all accomplished through family efforts and sacrifice. My brother, who became a medical doctor, completed his entire high school by correspondence. Our brothers related how they let him complete his assignments leaning against stooks (a bundle of sheaves stacked in a field) until called upon to unload the sheaves into a threshing machine. On completing high school, I likewise financed my university education. Interestingly, although our parents regretted not being in a position to assist their children with their schooling, no feelings of resentment were expressed by their children. We accepted the fact that we would have to do it on our own. My parents instilled the belief that self-help is a godly expectation. The Good Lord gave us talents, and expected us to develop these to the fullest.

Great successes are built on taking your negatives
and turning them into successes.

Summer Redstone in Forbes

Chapter Two
Formative Years

My mother Lydia was a warm and loving person who was very fond of her children. Even in the midst of the Depression, her heart went out to a single mother who had no way of supporting her son. Freddie entered my parents' home as a small foster child and brightened my mother's world. Events, however, altered this. Freddie's mother's status changed and she decided to reclaim her child. His departure left a great void in Lydia's world; one she felt would have to be filled.

With August's concurrence, she caught a train in the nearby village and set off for Winnipeg. There she contacted friends and a pastor. Her goal was to acquire a replacement for Freddie and her efforts eventually led her to an orphanage. There she became captivated by a blond, shy boy whose young mother's untimely death, preceded by a disintegrated marriage, led to his current status. His two older brothers were cared for by grandparents who could not take on additional financial responsibilities — hence an orphanage was the only alternative. The bond having been cemented, Lydia returned home to the farm with a new three-year-old family member. That person was me!

Without doubt this event had the greatest impact on my life. Had I not been adopted into this family my future would have developed quite

differently. For this I have always been truly grateful. For my parents, who already had seven children, to assume this additional responsibility during exceedingly hard times, was a remarkable act of self-sacrifice and love — a standard that was instilled in their children.

Anyone can be a heart specialist.
The only requirement is loving someone!
Angie Papadaki

Most child development experts tend to agree that early childhood experiences play a critical role in future development. Nothing stands out in my early home memories other than feelings of belonging. I suppose being so much younger than my siblings (the next to me was eight years older), I was like a family mascot. Family members, however, have not suggested that I was unduly indulged. My mother, coming from the old school, had a no-nonsense outlook on discipline — loving but firm. Her child-raising ideology can best be summed up in her expressed opinion that "The Good Lord has entrusted me with these children and some day I will be held accountable." This viewpoint became a basic child rearing philosophy guiding our child rearing practices. Interestingly, it is often quoted by my children — the third generation. My mother, who had little schooling, certainly had her priorities right — lots of love but consistent. It leads one to wonder whether too much theory gets in the way of effectiveness! So many, so-called schooled people have no concept of how to raise children and the end results are often tragic. I believe that my mother's approach markedly contributed to the success of her children, although some family members felt that she was somewhat harsh. She demanded complete adherence to commands with disobedience promptly chastised. Opportunities for self-expression were minimized. It certainly influenced my outlook on life.

My father, a quiet, reserved but highly intelligent man, left child-raising to his wife, but he was always there as a steadying, accepting influence. By nature he was a shy non-demonstrative person with few outward signs of affection. He seldom embraced his children, feeling uncomfortable with displays of fondness. He, nevertheless, cared deeply for his family. This was more than offset by my mother who was decidedly affectionate and freely displayed her feelings. This environment created security and established a firm base for individual development. A lack of financial resources was more than equalized by such surroundings — an ideal setting for my future growth and development.

Too many parents are not on spanking terms with their children.
Life's Little Instruction Book

Adoption was a very uncommon practice at that time. Indeed, it carried with it a certain stigma based on much misinformation and faulty beliefs. A common viewpoint was that inherited blood was responsible for behaviour and one could never know when bloodlines would make their presence felt. The assumption, of course, was that such influences would invariably be negative. An understanding of heredity and environment and how these interact, was an unfamiliar notion. This was especially so in a rural community where few residents completed more than a grade eight education — if that!

My mother earned little credit for taking in a child of questionable heritage. Being very confident, this had little impact on her. She was not swayed by public opinion! What was right was right. Lydia was very outspoken in her views, which often alienated her less insightful neighbours. She always attempted to insulate me from community biases, which she believed were based on ignorance. One must practice what one believes, was her guiding principle. The Good Lord cannot be deceived! This strong belief and protective nurturing provided a very secure environment for me, which persisted over time. I never felt I was any different from any other family member. In fact my siblings were extremely protective of me. Even though I was much shorter than my brothers, this was simply treated as a normal development requiring no additional explanation. Often it was suggested that, being the youngest, I couldn't compete at the trough at mealtime, which stunted my growth. This familial approach implanted solid feelings of security.

While I had a unique background compared to my siblings, my parents treated me the same. I was their child, they loved me, guided and disciplined me just as they did the other children. Being adopted required no special treatment.

Heredity is a splendid phenomenon that relieves us
of the responsibility for our shortcomings.

Doug Larson

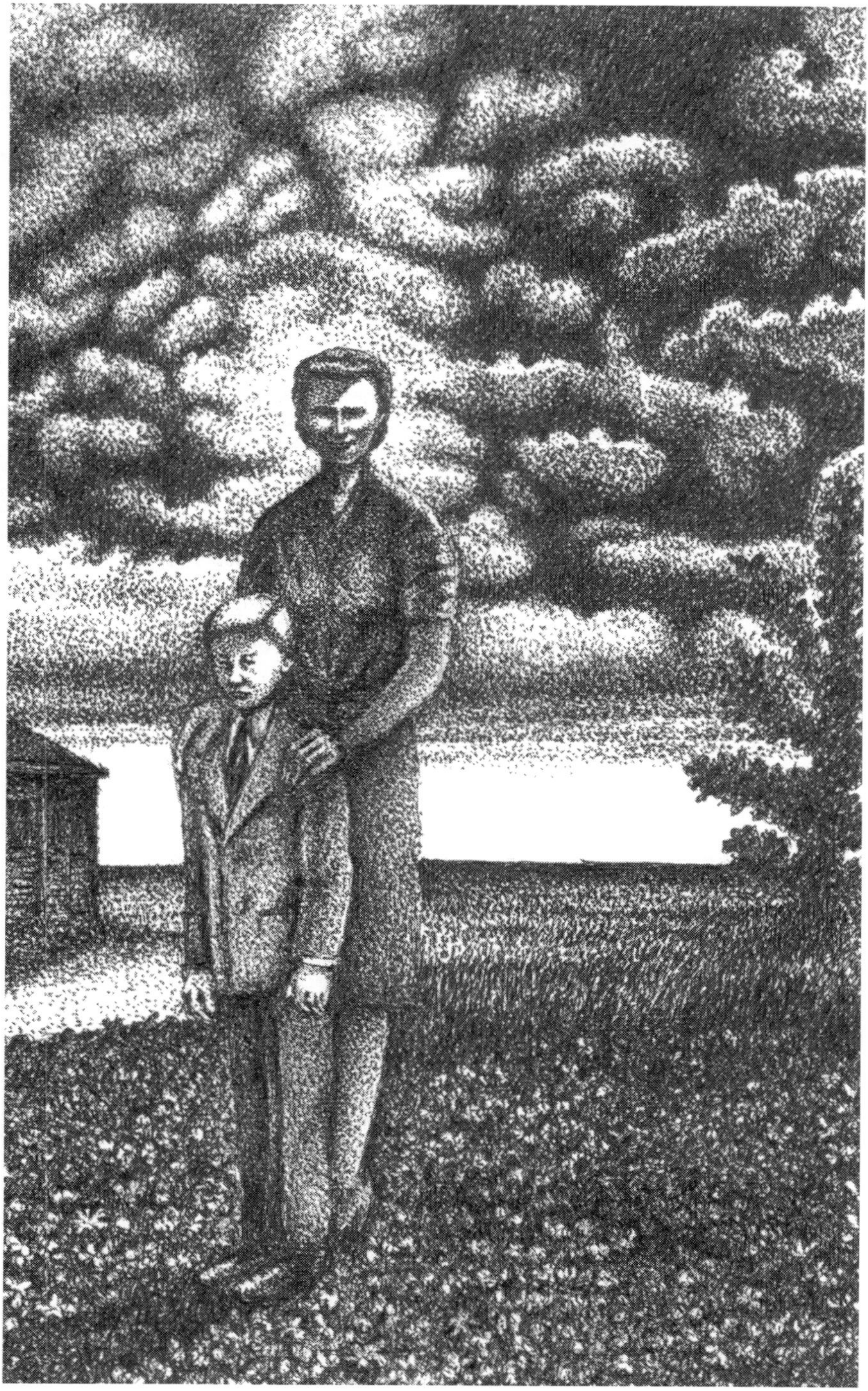

Chapter Three
My Community

My community was some five miles square and was made up of very similar people, mainly of German origin from various parts of Europe. With few exceptions, most were settlers with a background in farming wishing to escape oppressive, limiting conditions. Canada provided the hope of a promising future. They shared common traits: a willingness to work hard, simple expectations, with their lives centred around the local church and school. A common language and similar beliefs tied them together.

My early years in the 1930's, compared with today's North American world, could, in some ways, be viewed as primitive. Rarely, but only during very dry seasons, was a Model T Ford seen fighting rural ruts. Horse drawn wagons, buggies and democrats during the summer and sleighs during the winter were the usual mode of transportation. A few innovative folk enclosed cutters (small sleighs) which were heated by wood stoves with chimneys sticking through the top. The lines directing the horses were inserted through small holes making the interior quite snug. A hinged window in the front allowed a view of the cold outside. Larger versions were built to serve as school vans transporting children to school. Those driving the vans stayed inside the van all day, perhaps knitting, playing cards or story telling to pass the time away.

The existing lifestyle was preserved by a lack of modern conveniences. Indoor plumbing was non existent. The outdoor biffy served the necessities of life both winter and summer. As the weather cooled, stays were progressively shortened. Considerable attention had been focused on the status of a two holer compared to a one holer and the romance associated with a half moon or star carved in the door. It was here that pictures in the Eaton's catalogue of sleighs, toboggans, bicycles with a bell, whetted dreams of fancy. Halloween always launched acts of heroism directed at this princely abode. Toppling it confirmed one's manliness, especially if it belonged to the local teacher.

Today's society, robbed of electricity, would consider this a catastrophe. Yet access to such an unaccustomed resource was not seen as an essential requirement. Homes and public places were lit by coal oil and hissing kerosene lamps, which in fact created a cosy environment. Christmas trees lit by burning candles, carefully watched, accentuated the fragrance of evergreens.

My brothers, learning that electricity could be manufactured by windmills, decided to put this information to use. They erected a propeller, attached to a generator, on top of the barn, which they wired to a car battery inside. When the wind blew the batteries were charged and a single light bulb converted the barn into a fairyland, all smells being temporarily erased. Milking twenty cows by hand, without the aid of milking machines, was a common practice. A manually operated cream separator divided the milk from the cream, which was converted into butter or sold. The skim milk was fed to the pigs or young calves.

Household appliances today are operated almost exclusively by electricity. So also is the radio. In my youth a battery-operated radio was developed to fill this gap. Great excitement accompanied the arrival of this enriching device. Accessing the airwaves required the stringing of a long wire aerial between poplar trees. A twist of the knob opened a new and expanded world with Amos and Andy amusing us with their antics. Lux Radio Theatre Presents Hollywood introduced by Cecil B. DeMille, Monday evening at eight, was listened to in the dark, and opened worlds previously unknown! Childhood programs are still etched in my mind. These included Boston Blackie, The Green Hornet, The Shadow Knows All, Orphan Annie and, of course, The Lone Ranger.

Phones used in other communities were not available to us. Those having phones could contact a neighbour by, for example, ringing three long rings and one short with every client being assigned their code. Life frequently was enriched by eavesdropping on other peoples' conversations. One knew that others were listening in by the sound of heavy breathing, whispering, coughing, kids crying in the background or by the fact that one could no longer make oneself heard due to a weakened system.

In our community, the modern telephone was preceded by the barbed wire phone. Using coils, batteries and various equipment, conversations were sent along barbed wire fences connected by wires over road entrances. This worked well in the winter but the arrival of spring grounded the messages since many fences were nailed to trees. These early life experiences evoke many nostalgic memories.

The definition of the Golden Age of anything
is when you were there.
Justice Anthony M. Kennedy

Chapter Four
Life on the Farm and in the Community

Farming was a very toilsome task. Until the outbreak of World War II, tractors were rare and, if available, unaffordable. Land was cleared by hand. Teams of horses and occasionally powerful oxen, extracted trees whose roots had been exposed by physical labour applying pickaxe and shovels. Once cleared, the land was tilled by teams of horses pulling ploughs and harrows. Men frequently followed on foot — others rode on two wheeled carts. As a teenager I often walked barefoot behind the harrows to keep dirt out of my shoes. Wrestling an existence out of a quarter section of land, plus a rented quarter, was a formidable task. The limited income pried from the land was supplemented by selling eggs, chickens, pigs, cattle, and shipping cream preserved in the icehouse.

A high point on the farm occurred in the fall-harvest time. Individual farmers contracted with others to do the final harvesting since few farmers could afford threshing machines, which separated grain from straw. The arrival of the tractor-drawn threshing machine, hayracks and workers was a momentous event providing great opportunities for socializing. Tractors and, in some communities, steam engines, connected to threshing machines by long belts, drove the operation. Several teams loaded sheaves, previously dried in stooks, into hayracks to be fed into the threshing machine's mouth. Grain poured out of a spout into a storage granary. As these filled, children were given the task of shoveling grain into all corners up to the rafters. The straw, separated from the grain, was blown through a long pipe extending from the back of the threshing machine, to form large stacks — good hiding places for children. Threshing crews commenced operation at first light, if the grain was dry, and continued late into the night. Serving food provided ladies a golden opportunity to display their cooking skills. The aim was to surpass neighbourhood competition. Nothing was spared. A high point for children was to carry coffee and sweets to the crew mornings and afternoons; an uplifting experience comparable to taking part as an extra in a Hollywood movie. The departure of the threshing gang was a real emotional downer. Life once again returned to the ordinary.

> *What do Saskatchewan farmers do after the harvest?*
> *They eat all they can, then can what they can't.*
> *Quoted in* The Toronto Globe and Mail

While money was in short supply, there was always ample food. Although variety was limited, no one seemed to suffer from hunger. Canned food and breakfast cereal did not exist. The day started with a hefty helping of porridge, home-made bread or "Johnny Cake" made from cornmeal served on Sundays. A crackling wood stove, lit at dawn, cooked the food and heated the large kitchen. Water in pails used to make cocoa often froze in the winter since there was no heat at night. The similar makeup of the community produced a levelling effect — a common standard. We were all in the same boat. This being so, deprivation assumed a different dimension. For example, in the spring time children went barefoot to school to preserve shoes, a practice encouraged by the parents. The children, however, looked forward to this with anticipation since it announced the arrival of spring.

Childhood expectations, to a much greater extent than in today's society, were moderated by family resources. Children accepted this since few appetites and dreams had been developed. Nevertheless, I remember longingly admiring a tricycle beautifully displayed in the Eaton's catalogue, but dared not ask for such luxury. The expectation was that you made do with what was available. There simply was no surplus! This sprouted many self-made toys: guns carved out of tree branches, sleighs made from leftover two by fours, sling shots with which to harass birds, skis made from wooden barrel staves, home-made cradles, and hand driven ice cream makers turning thick farm cream into delicious ice cream. Pleasure was dependent on your own inventiveness. These experiences set the stage for the future — the ability to make the most of your immediate circumstances.

Rather than buy coffee, my mother roasted a mixture of grains comparable to present day Postum. The little hoard of real coffee, garnered over time, was squirreled away for use on special occasions such as visitations by the pastor. No family member dared ask for a second cup. Soap, yellow in colour, was made by boiling animal fat together with water in a large oval copper container called a boiler. To this mixture, lye was proportionally added. The resulting pungent smelling product, in addition to removing dirt, cleared sinuses and the first layer of skin if excessively applied. Sheep sheared in the springtime produced greasy, dirty wool that became white and soft when washed in this boiling soapy water. A toothy instrument, called a carder, served as a comb preparing the tangled wool for spinning. My mother spent many an evening at her foot-driven spinning wheel converting fluffy wool into yarn. As a young boy, I was often called upon to extend my arms, around which yarn was wound into skeins ready for knitting. Although luxuries were available only on festive occasions, there was never a shortage of basic foods such as meat, milk and vegetables since these were raised on the farm. Hired men were paid a dollar a day and worked from dawn until dusk. Bread by comparison, cost five cents a loaf but was seldom bought. An "Oh Henry" chocolate bar was a nickel as was a soft drink. A high point in my life was riding with my father in a horse drawn wagon to the nearest town ten miles distant. Here I was rewarded with a double header ice cream cone, which I nurtured as long as possible — a vivid memory that makes my mouth water and lingers on with me to this day.

> *In the old days, when things got rough, what you did was do without.*
> *Bill Copeland*

A revenue source for children was gopher tails. These squirrel-like animals were a hazard to farmers since they destroyed their grain. The government instituted an incentive program, similar to today's summer works projects, designed to keep these rodents in check. A cent a tail was paid for gopher tails, a goodly sum, which prompted innovative trapping strategies. Other revenue sources were explored. On my way to school, during the winter, I set snares on well-trodden rabbit trails. On my return at day's end I collected those caught. These I subsequently skinned and put on stretcher boards. Once dry, they sold for the tidy sum of a nickel. Weasels were especially sought after since they paid the princely sum of two dollars. This was equivalent to two days pay for a farm worker. I experienced a traumatic drop in my fortune when a weasel I caught was pilfered by the school bully who subdued me with threats of abuse if I complained. This helped prepare me for other financial setbacks in life.

Adversity and hard times generated creativity! People took advantage of the resources available to them. Chickens, turkeys, geese, lamb, beef and an occasional deer or moose were cut into small pieces and placed in sealers with salt and pickling spices. They were then processed on wood stoves, hours on end, until cooked and sealed. Since wood was plentiful, cost was not a factor. Guts were scraped clean and filled with ground beef, moose or deer and, of course, pork to keep the sausage moist. Herbs and spices and loads of garlic were added. Sausage rings and hams, previously soaked in brine, were hung in smokehouses stoked with green willows, carefully vented, to get the most smoke output. Once thoroughly smoked, they could be hung from rafters all summer without fear of deterioration. Fall saw mothers and children out in the woods picking raspberries, saskatoons, cranberries, which were canned, converted into jellies, jams, syrup and stored away. Chokecherries were especially prized. In addition to making good jelly and syrup, they, like dandelions, were easily converted into wine for those numerous festive seasons requiring a special bracer. Unexpected smells, many years later, stimulate many memories.

Hard physical labour day after day took its toll. Unlike today, people were old at sixty both physically and emotionally worn out. The aging process was advanced by ongoing worries such as the Depression and anxiety resulting from sons going off to war with no assurance they would ever return. The idea of a comfortable and secure retirement was a hypothetical concept at best. Family living, with all the associated problems, was the norm for the day.

In spite of everything, life on the farm provided unique opportunities for personal growth and development. Even as a young child and certainly as a teenager, you filled an important role in day to day operations. The six-year-old carried in split wood from the nearby wood pile, emptied small slop pails, plucked sprouts from potatoes in the root cellar, and brought in cows at milking time. As a thirteen-year-old, I cleaned barns, ran a tractor, stooked sheaves at harvest time and milked cows, to the tune of "You Are My Sunshine," sung with my harmonizing sister. During the summer I was given the tedious task of ensuring cattle did not stray into grain fields. Frequently, absorption in a western novel following the exploits of a gunslinger blocked out everything. Cattle took advantage of my preoccupation, to my mother's displeasure, which she reflected by burning my novel.

My contributions to the household made a difference and increased my importance. I was an essential, contributing member. If I dropped the ball, others were adversely affected and I was made aware of this. As such I, in my home environment, counted. I had personal worth and was appreciated even though this was infrequently expressed. Perhaps, regrettably, saying so was considered unnecessary!

Unfortunately, today's youngsters, through no fault of their own, are frequently denied similar vital growth opportunities. Their parents, often second-generation immigrant offspring, who had to struggle to make their mark, wish to insulate their children from similar life challenging experiences. In the process, they become over protective and end up throwing the baby out with the bath water. Certainly little is gained by subjecting children to the many painful survival experiences that their parents were obliged to endure. Over-reacting to the past, however, often leads to excessive indulgence, which fails to develop character. This process ensures fulfillment of the old proverb: from shirtsleeves to shirtsleeves in three generations.

Throughout life I have discovered that everything must be learned and the foundations for good development must begin early. This includes exposure to difficult challenges and experiences in a supportive and loving environment that allows one to test skills and aptitudes while at the same time developing an appreciation for the rights of others. Children, who are denied this, develop a distorted view of life and later experience difficulty adjusting to challenges. An undisciplined person is not a well-adjusted person! It would seem that caring, loving and insightful parents have an obligation to provide such developmental opportunities in a nurturing setting. My parents provided this.

Many of my early life experiences were hurtful and were not something I wished for my children. The love and support of my parents and my family, however, allowed these events to become learning experiences that helped equip me for future living. Even very traumatic childhood experiences, such as being jeered and bullied for being adopted, need not have long lasting destructive effects. The support of parents, family and friends, can convert sad events into a growth experience. This does not require a college education so much as a caring heart! My parents displayed such characteristics even though at the time I was unaware that this was so. Fortunately, my life experience enabled me to evaluate past events from a broader perspective.

Kind words are like honey-sweet to the taste and good for your health.
Proverbs 16:24

Life was more than an ongoing struggle for survival. Entertainment was self-made with little cost. Church was a common unifier with most in the community attending regular Sunday services. Visiting after church provided opportunities for gossiping and socializing. Various other activities were greatly enjoyed. Local accordion, guitar and violin players made barn dances a well attended event with enthusiasm exceeding dancing aptitude. Local swains strutted their best with performance enhanced by a reinforcing swig from a home-brew bottle hidden outside in a truck. Competition often resulted in a display of fisticuffs, which was an accepted form of problem solving. It certainly had the therapeutic value of clearing the air. Since there were no psychologists readily available, this probably served as a less costly and perhaps a more effective alternative.

Most people can work up a head of steam
without knowing what's cooking.
Quoted in The Toronto Globe and Mail

The community provided other life enriching experiences. The "Box Social" and "Pie Social" were such events. Ladies prepared box lunches and pies, which were then put up for auction. Admirers and potential beaux, who had done some sleuthing, then bid on the package. It was assumed that the lady who prepared the goodies would then spend the evening with the successful bidder. Competition became heated and continued until a competitor's resources were exhausted. Resentment at losing often showed itself in the loser letting the air out of the opponent's tires. This denied the competition the opportunity of driving home the date he had won in the bidding war.

A novel approach, that favoured the less well endowed ladies, was the "Shadow Social." Every lady who brought a box lunch played the game of hiding behind sheets strung on a line. To level the playing field, a light was shone on contestants who turned in such way as to project the most favourable profile. Thus heavy weights became slim and appealing and the skinny gained the desired pounds — a method that could well be adopted by "Weight Watchers." This process, however, baffled the bidding process frequently resulting in mismatches that failed to spark romance. Needless to say, many a young sport who misjudged became the object of considerable ribbing. It was not an activity for the faint hearted, male or female.

The community had its own set of values, which ranged from rather permissive to very rigid — depending on who did the judging. Bootlegging was not considered a criminal offence even though considered so by the RCMP. Rather, it provided a community service since few could afford store-bought booze. Periodically, those filling this need would be raided, appear in court and given the opportunity to rest their skills in a place of penance. This, however, failed to change occupational interests, demean the culprit, or reduce the client population. Similarly, at the annual school picnic, home-brew enhanced team support. When an occasional eye was blackened for perceived inappropriate remarks, a handshake and another pull at the flask re-established good relations. For most, this was an acceptable solution.

I have taken more good from alcohol
than alcohol has taken from me.

Winston Churchill

What was especially interesting was people's capacity to separate thinking from their behaviour. Church attendance and choir singing, done with great gusto, was one thing and school picnic behaviour another. This discrepancy never seemed to become apparent or alter individual behaviour nor was such conflicting behaviour interpreted as phoney. After all, one must let off steam! Man has a tremendous capacity for insulating lip service from behaviour — a lesson that well prepared me for the inconsistencies of life. Values, unless taught early, seldom make their appearance in later life. Many have argued that the likelihood of changing human behaviour diminishes rapidly with age. One southern gentleman said it so aptly when he commented that: "you can teach an old dog new tricks but you got to whop 'im."

As a youngster one knew community standards and reacted accordingly. Although quite restrictive by today's judgements community expectations, rigidly enforced, provided a degree of security, a rudder, guiding behaviour and a feeling that someone cared about you. Ambiguity and confusion was minimized a toss-up between rights and responsibility. In today's society, we seem to have swung in the opposite direction. Chastising someone's child for an obvious anti-social act often initiates a very negative parental response supplemented by the threat of legal action. In the process, the child's behaviour is reinforced, leading to future adjustment problems. Society is not nearly as tolerant as are parents.

Sadly, in today's world, a hug from a teacher or a coach is avoided because of the threat of sexual abuse. When I was a child, such demonstrations of support however, greatly enhanced confidence building. As we grow older, there exists the tendency to withdraw into our own little secure world. People drive up to their homes, push a button that opens the garage door, drive in, close the door and retreat inside. Yet one of the common contributors to poor physical and mental health is loneliness, the feeling of isolation that no one really cares. In the process one's self-worth and capacity to address one's needs is eroded. To reach out for sustenance is risky since it carries with it the prospects of rejection, something we all wish to avoid.

> *The common curse of mankind — folly and ignorance.*
> *William Shakespeare*

Communities of the day seemed to have a greater capacity to absorb the disadvantaged and eccentric. There were several in my community who were clearly disabled. Neighbours tolerated their quirks, kept an eye open for them and ensured that no harm came their way. One old bachelor was somewhat disturbed but managed to survive on his own. He, like the prophets of old, had noteworthy dreams, which the local newspaper published and were read with considerable interest. The following week, he provided his interpretation of the dreams, which were even more avidly consumed. On another occasion, he erroneously concluded that pictures in the female section of the Eaton's catalogue were of women you could order as a potential mate. Needless to say, when he received his package of women's underwear he was quite disappointed.

Quirkiness must have run in the family. His brother had a farm nearby and saw himself as a bit of an advanced thinker not unduly influenced by local knowledge and experience. Each year he attempted to get a head start on farming. He planted his crop too early only to have it freeze and require replanting — a costly mistake. He built a device consisting of a large mounted rotary saw with a movable frame on which logs could be placed. By moving the frame back and forth, smaller chunks of wood could be cut to fuel kitchen stoves. One day, once again beating the gun, he got up when it was still dark. Not being sure of the day's activity and how much fuel he would need, he lit a match, looked into the gas tank and almost blew off his head. On another occasion, as I came by to pick up his son on the way to school, he chased me off his yard with a broomstick. He was annoyed that I had previously contradicted him when he came to the school and made false accusations against the teacher. In my dreams I still look behind me for that swinging broomstick. No wonder children develop neurotic behaviour that only hefty doses of Ritalin can alleviate. Perhaps they also were similarly pursued in their past. This was an early, needed, learning experience in the art of giving timely statements. Offering contradictory opinions can be hazardous.

Another bachelor, Cornelius, became an idol of mine. The Beatles, had they existed then, would have played second fiddle to him. His esteem was rooted in his appearance on a local radio show singing western tunes, which he accompanied on a Hawaiian guitar. He always treated my interest in music with respect and spoke knowledgeably about things I didn't know. Talking to a star, who treated me kindly, was a heady experience that greatly strengthened my self worth. I had arrived! It mattered less that his esteem was not broadly based. What was important was my perception of him and his acceptance of me. Too often we downgrade what is important to a child since, in our eyes and our experience, we know it is unwarranted. In the process, we demean the child when nothing is gained by doing so. I'm sure my siblings smirked at my devotion but they made no attempt to correct me.

Everybody has to be somebody to somebody to be anybody.
Malcolm S. Forbes

My mother regularly sent me to Cornelius' place with a two-quart jar of sauerkraut in payment for a hair cut. My hero had other characteristics of which I was unaware until drawn to my attention later in life. He treated his chickens like kinfolk. They visited with him in his shack and at night would roost at the end of his bed on the rung connecting the bedposts. In the fall he decapitated the chickens. Rather than pluck the feathers, he threw them into the granary for cold storage. There they remained, frozen, until he had a yen for chicken soup. When so inclined, he thawed a chicken and plucked and cleaned it. This was a non-traditional approach that obviously worked for him and which Campbell Soups might well adopt as a cost saver. His creativity and inventiveness was not restricted to making chicken soup. According to tales told by a brother, he briefly fired up his Fordson tractor with gas generated by converting coal into coke. Unfortunately, an explosion terminated the invention. I still think fondly of him, especially the courtesy he extended me. As I reflect on this, the importance that timely recognition played in my life cannot be over-emphasized — we all need to feel important if we are to achieve our potential! It is interesting to note that worthy recognition sources vary markedly through various stages in our development. What impressed us as a teenager no longer has relevance as we grow older — some adults however become frozen in time.

A man of stature has no need for status.
Charles Hendrickson Brower

The local country store was a central gathering point similar to todays pub, but without booze. It embraced a unique host of somewhat conflicting smells; binder twine, coal oil, harness, mothballs, bananas, apples, peppermints and blue jeans all wrapped together by the smell of oil-soaked wooden floors. People gathered to collect their mail. This frequently included the Eaton's parcel — the lifeline of the community. Men huddled around the stove in mid-winter dressed in mackinaws and felt boots enclosed in rubbers. Accurate stove spitting produced hissing sounds that added to the conversation of the day as they waited for the train — the prime reason for the gathering. The engineer announced the train's arrival with three long toots, as it seemed to careen around the bend. Long horizontal arms connected five-foot high wheels, which moved rhythmically as they propelled the train ahead. Steam and smoke enveloping the engine seemingly magnified its immense power. Horses tied to poles, some distance away, often reared up on their hind legs intimidated by the over-powering presence. The fireman lowered a large metal protected hose from the water tank quenching the thirsty beast. Passengers embarked and disembarked, freight, mail and deliveries were quickly transacted. A toot or two, a wave at the gathering, wheels slipping on the rails and the train quickly disappeared into the horizon. The high point of the day had come to an end! Left behind were smouldering cinders and occasionally a flattened penny that an adventuresome boy had placed on the track in advance. Those gathered returned to the store, which also served as a post office, to collect what had been delivered.

Locals had little respect for the storekeeper's private life. When they wanted something they wanted it now. Consequently, raps on the window after midnight for desired supplies were commonplace and were generally acceptable. The proprietor also functioned as a local financier. During off-season, before crops were sold, purchases were obtained on credit. Running tabs were kept and redeemed when monies became available. Some were better at acquiring goods than repaying debts. This was treated as part of the cost of doing business.

I don't lend money because it causes amnesia.
Mack McGinnis

Villages were some nine miles apart, which was the maximum distance people could travel by horse and wagon to deliver their produce. The advent of cars changed things and led to community restructuring and the disappearance of such hamlets. Former thriving villages were relegated to history. When, as an adult, I returned to the nearby village of my youth, where my brother had once run a store, all that remained were a few boarded up buildings and a sign bravely marking the past. The former grain elevator, the train station, that once were central to the community, were all gone. When I revisited the farm site of my childhood I was equally distressed. The trees that had formerly dotted the landscape and were imprinted on my mind were no longer there. Even the buildings were gone except bits of the barn. The church nearby that my father had so painstakingly built, was no longer in use with windows cracked and steps leaning awkwardly. I experienced sadness over what time had destroyed — the destruction of my memories, I was overcome with nostalgia. This place evoked so many recollections, both good and bad. But I also discovered that I had grown to the point that I had subordinated the bad and primarily recalled the good. Human nature has such a wonderful way of insulating us from past pains. This is especially the case if subsequent adjustments have enabled us to put past feelings into a broader global focus. So many painful memories that moulded our behaviour are best put to rest if we are to be freed up from their impact and move on. Revisiting one's former community, even though it has changed, helps address past hurts and provides closure.

Why is it that the things you most clearly remember
are the things you want most to forget?
Blake McAdam

Chapter Five
Early School Years

My school was painted yellow with a bright red roof. As a small child it seemed very large. Perhaps, being a place of learning increased its size. A boot scraper dominated the entrance and its use was a requirement. As one entered, a small cloakroom to the left was for the girls and the one to the right was the boy's domain. Double desks faced the chalkboard to the front. Located in the centre rear was a large barrel-like stove mounted on its side on stilts. This was surrounded by sheet metal to protect the unwary wrestlers proving their strength and ingenuity prior to the teacher's arrival. The wood floor soaked with oil, the traditional treatment, was the permeating smell that hit you as you entered the school. The front wall was covered by a pitted grey-green blackboard. A low shelf attached to the board held chalk and erasers for both student and teacher use. A tray of gelatin (Hektograph) on which a coloured stencil was pressed, imprinted the design. Paper placed on top and gently stroked provided the means for reproducing some twenty to thirty copies — an early photocopier. This, other than chalk, was the school's only instructional equipment.

Class instruction was frequently interrupted by a hand held high to gain permission to visit the boys' or girls' outdoor biffy. Frequent visitations were made by the less academically inclined. Drinking water came from a nearby well on a farmer's yard. Two students, selected on a rotational basis, carried the water back to the school in an open pail taking as much time as possible. An aluminum dipper, used by the entire class, satisfied student thirst. Sanitary worries were a concern of sissies.

Extracurricular activities included spelling bees where two teams struggled to outperform rivals. At day's end, the teacher often read several pages from an ongoing novel, which whetted my appetite for reading. I read the entire school library of six books in short order. Few reading materials were available at home with the exception of the local prairie newspaper. This included comics, stimulating romantic novels — secretly read — and a Loving Hearts column for those in search of a marriage partner.

Grades one to eight were taught in the same room with several students in each grade — the forerunner of today's open room concept. Some years teachers changed at mid term. Others had only a year's Teachers College training. By the time you reached grade eight you knew the course of studies having heard it for eight years.

Students in the younger grades made miniature tractors and wagons from plasticine. The older boys constructed toy buildings using willow sticks cut from schoolyard bushes. There were few special activities for girls other than hopscotch. Most extracurricular activities were self-generated. This included "anti-I-over," which involved throwing a ball over the schoolhouse to be caught by the team on the other side who then came running around the school trying to eliminate an opposing team member by hitting him/her with the ball. Success produced a score of one — a miss lost a point.

The school had a well-worn softball, softened over time, and a battle scarred bat both put to use by scrub teams picked by choosing from the school membership. There were stars and then there were losers who were chosen when no one else was left. Periodically, the best players took on another school team some five miles away. Those participating walked the distance to and fro but victories, glorified by the community, made it all worthwhile.

Winter introduced a change of pace with a form of hockey played by both boys and girls. A small slough, nearby, was hand cleaned for use. A few players had skates, some stuffed with paper, to make them fit, but most youngsters played in moccasins and felt boots. Frozen horse buns served as pucks. A few store-bought hockey sticks graced the rink in contrast with the hand-hewn sticks carved out of willow branches. While hockey was the game, the focus of many players was to destroy the fancy hockey sticks — a hated status symbol.

Some children walked several miles to school (up hill both ways) carrying their lunch and cocoa in a corked liniment bottle which was frozen by the time they arrived at school. Corks in bottles placed around the stove began popping near noon signalling the arrival of lunchtime. Teacher's authority and control was reinforced by the presence of a rubber strap in the teacher's desk drawer meant for use. A strapping by the teacher often was followed by comparable discipline at home. Parent teacher sessions were unheard of. On one occasion a parent and an older brother unjustly accosted the teacher for the supposed mistreatment of the school bully. He apparently had messed his pants and blamed the teacher for his dilemma. The complaints were resolved through fisticuffs with the teacher winning the match. No more was heard of the episode. I was overjoyed with the outcome since the bully previously had stolen the weasel I had trapped!

The whole educational system was shored up by the school inspector who appeared, without warning, at least once yearly to observe teacher and student performance. No one commanded more respect and fear than a school inspector did. He must have had special vision to make an accurate evaluation during such a short spying session. At least the appearance of academic proficiency was created.

In an unschooled community, impressed with authority, that carried the day.

Many might well judge this to be an ineffective educational system. Nevertheless, a surprising number of successful businessmen and professional people were produced. One study conducted in the Maritimes concluded that as many successful people came out of that system as in today's technically supported approach. The ones who suffered most were those of limited ability or handicapped in other ways. It does make one question today's heavy reliance on capital equipment as a major teaching tool. Generating a hunger for learning, regardless of how generated, seems to be a primary component. This relies heavily on the development of student/teacher interpersonal relationships that inspire students to test their potential in a supportive environment. Mechanical devices generate little warmth! The teachers who made the greatest impact on me were those with whom I was comfortable — those who made me feel worthy — who encouraged me to try my best without the threat of embarrassment or worry about failure.

A major factor contributing to school success was parental involvement. While parents probably were no more effective than today, at least teachers were not as encumbered by unruly kids. Children were there to learn — or else. Perhaps restrictive, the learning process at least was not derailed by delinquent behaviour so often a major concern of today's educators.

Reading and writing, arithmetic and grammar do not constitute education any more than a knife, fork and spoon constitute dinner.
John Lubback

Starting school in any setting can be an intimidating experience. A one-room school offering eight grades in itself was quite an educational challenge. Teachers with qualifications just higher than their students often were peppered with requests demanding answers at the same time.

Individual insecurities and special needs were assigned low priority. Survival often was the teachers' main goal. Students were left largely to fend for themselves, especially during recess and lunchtime. In this environment, unless a bloodied nose forced an intervention, the school bully was king in the schoolyard. More times than not, fear of bully retribution silenced those hurt. My older sister, in grade eight, saw me through the first year and then I was on my own.

Poor school performance magnified feelings of insecurity. In fact, consideration was given to my repeating grade one since I wasn't up to class standards. My public school grades were not impressive. Mathematical concepts and rudiments of grammar were never grasped and little assistance was provided in overcoming these deficiencies. An older, very bright, brother when asked for help, intimidated me by expressing puzzlement at my lack of understanding. Consequently, being made to feel stupid, I stopped asking anyone for help. This lack of foundation knowledge became an on-going limitation.

Being one of the smallest, I became easy fodder for abuse. Community parental perceptions of my family background were readily passed on to their children who saw this as just grounds for my mistreatment, both physically and emotionally. For example, accusations that my birth mother had been a woman of questionable character, who had simply abandoned me, were frequently made. These were extremely hurtful, in fact devastating! Possible retribution against the abuser was neutralized by threats that my parents would be told demeaning stories about me. Hearing these, I assumed they would have no choice but to return me to the orphanage. Physical abuse, although painful, was not nearly as injurious. Fear, uncertainty and perhaps shame, prevented my sharing such hurts with my parents or family members.

Anxiety was a dominant emotion in my life. I remember arriving home after a troublesome day at school looking for my mother who wasn't in the house. Panic stricken, I ran from building to building searching for her.

If she were gone, I was lost and my return to the orphanage could happen. Overwhelming relief permeated when I found her.

Such hurtful recollections remain vivid to this day. As a young child, I simply didn't have the capacity to sort out fact from fiction. I merely accepted what was said. My family's day to day demanding domestic concerns, understandably, assumed priority. Subtle changes in their children's behaviour, prompted by personal anxieties, went by unnoticed. After all, children are always pouting about something and all would be back to normal shortly. Had someone asked about my change in mood, I probably would have poured out my heart. This merely emphasizes the importance of regularly taking time out to talk to one's children, to check how the day has gone, to provide opportunities for giving expression to hurts when they can be dealt with in a timely way.

The mere fact that I still reflect on these episodes with considerable feeling serves to emphasize how long lasting childhood experiences are — both good and bad. Fortunately, even though I kept these hurts to myself, the impact of such community abuses was offset by the ongoing love of my parents, especially my mother — a very demonstrative and loving person. Retreating to my home was the safe haven I needed — a place of healing. Nevertheless, such formative experiences very much influenced my future behaviour. Such episodes impact strongly on one's development even though one may not consciously be aware of this. I recall thinking, with considerable feeling that some day I would be successful, and then would come back and show everyone — sort of rub their noses in my achievements. When I could do so, it ceased to matter. The people involved in those early events no longer were of consequence. Nevertheless, these childhood experiences undoubtedly strongly influenced my desire to succeed.

Fortunately, family support and key role models encountered along the way helped offset early negative life experiences and put them into perspective. Without these moderating influences, I could easily have become bogged down by past animosities. Certainly all that happened to me provided insights no Psychology class could have imparted. Such formal training, built on what I had experienced, made me more understanding of others. But there are less traumatic ways of acquiring such knowledge!

Expecting the world to treat you fairly
because you are a good person is a little like expecting the
bull not to attack you because you are a vegetarian.
Dennis Wholey

The early school years, however, did offer good restorative opportunities, which strengthened my personal worth and offset demeaning experiences. I must have been a bit of a performer with fair reading skills, which I probably exploited to the fullest. The annual Christmas concert was one of the big events of the year. Preparing for the concert introduced me to the gramophone driven by a hand-cranked spring with a steel needle that periodically skipped as it followed the grooves on a Bakelite disk. The mesmerizing tune of "The Parade of the Wooden Soldiers," (the first recorded music I ever heard), set the pace as we marched in tune back and forth in true soldierly fashion. Perhaps this set the stage for my eventual entry into the military. No recording played on the best modern day equipment has made such an indelible musical impact on me. Observing my grandchildren march back and forth emphasizes how much music is a natural component of man — an avenue for self-expression — that deserves encouragement.

A week before the concert, the schoolroom, with the ingenuity of local craftsmen, was transformed into a fairyland. A stage was erected at the front of the school with bed sheets serving as stage curtains. Hours of practice transformed us into seasoned actors robed in homemade costumes. On the night of the performance, the entire community was there to bask in the reflected glory of their children's presentations. The atmosphere was electrifying! In this heady environment I experienced the thrill associated with being a star. From all the cast, the teacher chose me to be the master of ceremonies — the one who stood in front of the bed sheets introducing each classic event. My cup literally ran over. For that moment I was a person of consequence. Best of all, my parents were there. My mother's subsequent praise of my gala performance elevated me to the stars. All feelings of unworthiness were forgotten — no one could steal this moment from me! I had proven myself and my performance was recognized by those who counted. A lasting memory.

Lack of something to feel important about is
almost the greatest tragedy a man may have.
                                   Arthur E. Morgan

Chapter Six
The Church and the Community

A primary community unifier was the church, which, like the school, permeated every aspect of life. This was strengthened by the similar nature of the community — Germanic and Lutheran. Most activities centred around the school and the church with somewhat overlapping functions. We went to regular school five days a week and Saturday mornings attended Saturday school where we were taught Religion and German using the "Pfiebel" as a text. To some old timers in the community, God was German! Even as a youngster I sympathized with the pastor who was expected to teach the rudiments of German to students whose command of English, taught weekly at school, remained limited by a general lack of aptitude. My main concern was not pity for the pastor but prompted by the desire to complete these sessions as painlessly and as quickly as possible. With this in mind, and with cheeky confidence, I offered to assist the pastor by having some read their assignments to me. The pastor, who had been falling asleep with his chin resting on his hand supported on his knee, surprisingly agreed and the sessions were shortened. Both our pains were reduced. It's amazing the brass one musters up as a youth! Perhaps also, one tends to underestimate the insightfulness of a child. I probably sensed that this was all boring and tiresome to the pastor — any escape was welcomed.

I developed a special affection for the church since it, with the assistance of local help, was built by my father. I have vivid memories going back to the age of ten carrying his lunch to him in a syrup pail, to where the church was being built, a mile from our home. Daily, I remember looking forward with anticipation to the progress made as the church rose heavenward.

My father, a perfectionist carpenter and cabinetmaker, proceeded only once detailed plans had been developed. Accuracy was his guiding principle. For example: he carefully researched the scriptures to determine the directions Moses received for the construction of the Arc of the Covenant, as described in the Old Testament. Accordingly, he imported acacia wood for the construction of the altar, pulpit and baptismal font. Power tools being non-existent, great skill, care, and patience were required in their completion.

The final challenge was the erection of the steeple, involving the entire community, and the incorporation of a church bell rung during various festive occasions. If rung during weekdays, it meant someone had died. On the day of church installation my father, as the builder, assumed a special role in the dedication process. This recognition made me very proud!

After many years, the church has gone the way of time, neglected and no longer in use. Prior to its ending, I successfully convinced the church elders that it was only appropriate that some memento should stay with the family. In due course they agreed and transported the carefully packaged baptismal font to me. On its arrival, I felt that my father had entered my home — an emotional moment!

A man travels the world over in search of what
he needs and then returns home to find it.

George Moore

Church traditions, carried over from Europe, were perpetuated. I could never understand why the men sat in pews on the left of the church and women to the right especially when married couples shared the same bedroom. Children, six and over segregated by sex, sat up front and were rigidly controlled by a fierce elder. He, during the service, would go forward and grinding his false teeth severely tugged the ear of a disturber. To this day when I sit in church and hear movement behind me I cringe anticipating the arrival of a gnarled hand. My brother played the foot pumper organ accompanied occasionally by a choir dominated by a lady with an overpowering voice, which she exercised in a vibrato fashion. During my early childhood, lengthy sermons were conducted first in German and then repeated in English. The focus was on the sinfulness of man whom God would punish. Love and forgiveness seemed to assume secondary importance. God, instead of reflecting love and care, became an intimidating figure for me. Surely an appropriate balance would have been better!

> *If God believed in today's permissiveness,*
> *he would have given us the ten suggestions!*
> *The Orben Comedy letter*

At the outbreak of war the German services were stopped. At no time, however, did I feel any anti-German sentiment. This likely was due to the composition of the community. In fact, the war for many provided the opportunity to escape from the humdrum of everyday life. At the outbreak of the war, during July first celebrations, great excitement was caused by the arrival of an army scout car driven by soldiers. Shortly thereafter, several young men in the community enlisted and appeared in uniform at the Sunday church service, admired by all. Being tied into a large organization such as the military was a heady, uplifting experience. A big leap from the ordinary to the romantic and heroic. Some of those who left on a wave of glory failed to return. Others, who did, never quite adjusted to the life they had left behind. This was reflected in incidents of alcoholism and marriage break up. Surely all stages in life require preparation for living, if one attempts to return or recapture the past.

The influence of the church permeated my home and formed the basis of family life. The usual family and domestic conflicts still occurred but were dealt with in a more loving and forgiving way. Both parents were strong personalities and clashes did occur. My mother, highly emotional but very loving, was balanced by a reasoned, perhaps non-demonstrative husband and father. My mother, although unschooled, was very bright and her intelligence was enhanced by strength of character. Both she and my father had a strong faith, which they imparted to all their children. Ongoing church involvement strengthened this. My mother loved her children but did not overlook their deficiencies. As a child I felt she was rather harsh. This perception was fostered by the stinging reminder of pain inflicted on my bottom for misdemeanors. In retrospect, I feel it was done with love and the conviction that the Good Lord expected her to be a responsible parent who took action when needed.

In spite of her disciplinary practices, Mother never hesitated to shower love and praise especially when merited. At the church Christmas concert I overheard her proclaim to other ladies that I was the only one who made no mistakes and could be understood by all. Similarly, at the age of fourteen, at my class confirmation at church, my mother once again commented that I was the only one whose performance was error free. The fact that I still clearly recall these episodes with great fondness serves to emphasize how important parental love and support is in the development of a person. This was especially driven home to me by an episode involving our seven-year old grandson, whom we were taking out for the evening. As we were leaving, his father ran to the car and through an open window kissed his son. As we were driving away our grandson turned to us and commented, "My father has such a love for me."

Man's ingenuity shows no limits when it comes to showing off one's brilliance. This was well exemplified in the comments of another grand-child. I had previously been playing with him and cautioned him to take extra care in not banging my eye so as not to dislodge an implant, the result of cataract surgery. He was fascinated by what I told him and was only too ready to explain such surgery to his grandmother when asked to do so. This he did surprisingly well with great self-assurance and gusto. When complimented on his description and asked if he was going to be a doctor he commented, "No, I am smart and I'm strong." His father being a doctor, this response provided grist for future teasing. At least the criteria for an effective physician had been determined.

Teach a child how he should live and he will remember all his life.
Proverbs 22:6

Chapter Seven
Shoring Up One's Self

As a youngster, I grabbed reflected glory wherever I could. The natural resource is your immediate family. At the time, I had an older sister who was a nurse, one a schoolteacher and a brother a pastor. No one in the district had such a pedigree and I adopted it as my own. When my pastor brother came home and was invited to preach with the entire community in attendance, I could scarcely be pried from his side. My brother had status and since I was his brother, so did I. During the war the same brother entered the services as a chaplain with the rank of Captain. Another was a Provost Sergeant. I knew that no one in the community had siblings who had risen to such dizzy heights. Again my personal image was enhanced through association. One tends to under-emphasize the importance of role models early in life, both good and bad. Furthermore, the often-made erroneous assumption is that children only copy positive attributes while both are indiscriminately learned. I was especially fortunate to have been blessed with good examples that influenced me in many ways. Certainly these played a major role in my development.

On another occasion I developed a profound respect for my father who heretofore I respected because he was my father not because he possessed any unusual qualities. This was markedly changed when I listened to a conversation between my father and the pastor after dinner at our house. My father was being asked for advice and guidance. Heady stuff! He must be smart otherwise the wise pastor would not seek his opinion. Since my father was smart so also I had something going for me. This was further reinforced when the pastor asked my father to read the Sunday sermon during his absence. The fact that my father's monotone delivery was ridiculed by some in no way changed my perception. He had been singled out and that was all that mattered, and through association, I was important. I strongly believed that he was the smartest father in the district. This also set me above those who chose to put me down.

> *We cannot all be great, but we can always*
> *attach ourselves to something that is great.*
> *Harry Emerson Fosdick*

At school I was equally good at focusing attention on myself. The usual model for boys, on completion of grade eight, was to take up smoking, quit school, go to work and become a man. Aspiring to high school elevated me to the heights of an intellectual. Having shot off my mouth, I had no choice but to proceed. Needless to say, family role models and parental influence played a major role in my public utterances. Had such models been negative, the outcome would have been quite different. Even as a young child I quickly evaluated and used what would enhance my esteem — a not uncommon human characteristic. This became an established habit pattern. Feeling good about yourself, within limits, greatly influences aspirations. Feeling secure and important plays such a vital role in a child's life. This was consistently provided not only by my parents but also by my siblings who still lived at home on the farm at that time. I mattered, I had personal worth. Being a contributing member, I gained the additional affection of my siblings.

An example of this was one Sunday when my parents went off in a buggy to visit some neighbours. The understanding was that my older brother and I would do the chores. This included milking the cows, separating the milk, feeding the animals, etc. To earn brownie points with my brother, I started early. By the time he appeared, late in the evening, the work was done. Needless to say he was elated. He showed his appreciation by taking me back to a party he had reluctantly left. Being the only teenager there I felt I had achieved maturity. I was flying high and the love for my brother was strengthened.

The average guy spends much of his life trying to prove he isn't.
Toronto Globe and Mail

The completion of public school, leaving a secure one room setting, was a turning point in my life. My older siblings demonstrated that education provided a door to an expanded world. A sister whom I admired, a nurse, came home from the city on vacation and her descriptions of what she did excited me. Another had attained a teaching certificate. One brother was a pastor and another was attending university. These were powerful role models who served as inspiration sources for me — someone to imitate.

Early life experiences probably set the stage for my career choices. As a young person I recall wondering why some people seemed to take pleasure in abusing others. The study of human behaviour was a natural outgrowth of this thinking. Such early events could be compared to an in-depth course in sensitivity training, an awareness that has greatly helped me in life. Certain things have to be experienced. They cannot be taught. How sweet is sugar? You must taste it to know!

Your joy is your own; your bitterness is your own.
No one can share them with you.
Proverbs 14:10

Choosing education as the vehicle for self-enhancement, following in the footsteps of my siblings, obliged me to continue my schooling. In mid-winter, I emerged from under a feather tick into a frigid, dark environment. Hitting the floor was like contacting an ice block. Wood stoves were unlighted during the night because of the fear of fire. I wolfed down my porridge, climbed on my horse Jack, and rode bareback two miles to connect with the horse drawn, enclosed and heated sleigh mounted van. The nearest high school was another five miles with brief stops along the way for children.

Day's end saw the process reversed arriving home after nightfall. Car transportation, in the summer, improved the situation. While adults might see this as burdensome, I saw it as being rather exciting. Perceptions of a child are so different.

The high school, consisting of two rooms, was rather intimidating. I knew no one and those in attendance had long established friendships, which excluded me. Furthermore, I was poorly prepared academically and the long rides back and forth to school left no time for study. Consequently, I soon fell behind! The teacher changed in mid year and the replacement, a Scottish lady who taught French with a Scottish accent, added to my confusion. Her approach to Algebra further served to confound me.

The lack of foundation preparation, especially in math and writing was an ongoing impediment. Poor grades reinforced feelings of academic incompetence and led me to conclude I was not very bright and was only deluding myself to think otherwise. It took many years and success in other areas to offset this deprecating self-evaluation. These early home, school, church and community experiences became the filter through which I saw life as I left for broader horizons.

If you find a path with no obstacles,
it probably doesn't lead anywhere.

Frank A. Clark

A Journey Through Inadequacy

Chapter Eight
Leaving a Secure Environment

As a teenager, I fondly dreamt of leaving the farm. Looking back with less emotional involvement, it is safe to say my wish to leave was prompted by a variety of factors unknown to me at the time. Undoubtedly, a desire to escape many of the unpleasant memories associated with my childhood was a major inducement. I could never escape the fact that, due to my heritage, I was different, an enigma, and an oddity. This was reinforced by curiosity driven adult questions about my past family connections. They asked if attempts had been made by them to contact me. More tactless questions related to how I felt about being adopted. I hated such intrusions and I hated the people for asking and felt I had no way of striking back. Leaving was an option.

But it was more than that. I remember while looking for cows on horseback, romanticizing about life in the city. A totally unreal fantasy based on bits and pieces of information selectively gleaned from comments made by some of my siblings. These became realities for me. I dreamt about walking down city streets past stores radiating excitement that far exceeded life on the farm as I saw it. Compared to the town nearby, this was certainly true. This distortion, naively arrived at, undoubtedly far surpassed the boredom of farm life I was experiencing and set the stage for my departure.

My parents' advancing years and deteriorating health prevented their continuing on the farm. My father expressed the hope that with maturity and his assistance, I could develop into a farmer — something I only wished to escape! An older brother, having recently married, was ready and willing to take over the farm and could do so without additional preparation. This set the stage for my parents' retirement in Winnipeg and the launching of a new way of life for me. I had no idea what was facing me. Glamorized misconceptions filled my head. I had never been to a city. My closest exposure to urban living was contacts with the nearby town, infrequently visited. The decision had been made and plans were put into place to accommodate this.

The sale of the farm to my older brother merely generated three thousand dollars in 1944 funds — hardly enough for my parents to retire in an expensive city. An older single sister, a nurse, had carefully stashed away money for a rainy day. This she put to good use buying a small, relatively new house in a good community. She made this available to my parents, at no cost, so they could enjoy their retirement years. Such generosity not only enriched my parents' retirement, but also had a great impact on my future since it brought me to the city. The income generated from the sale of the farm and old age pensions, reluctantly accepted, were my parents' only source of revenue. This was supplemented by produce from my brother's farm. Nevertheless, they lived comfortably within their resources. Life in the city for my parents, in many ways, was a return to what they had previously experienced on arrival from Europe prior to financial setbacks necessitating relocation to the farm. They renewed membership in their original church where some old friends still worshipped. Numerous visits by their children during festive and other occasions enriched their lives. Summers were spent on the farm with their children and grandchildren, where they made useful contributions. These added meaning to their lives. Indeed, retirement proved to be a fulfilling experience for them.

The old order changeth, yielding place to new.
And God fulfills Himself in many ways,
Lest one good custom should corrupt the world.

Lord Tennyson

My parents' retirement and relocation greatly changed my life. The plan was for them to remain on the farm until crops were harvested in late September or early October. School, however, started the first week of September. Consequently, arrangements were made for me to proceed to the city ahead of my parents. This generated mixed feelings of excitement and apprehension. The fantasies were being put to the test and I wasn't at all sure I was up to it.

I had often observed train arrivals in our village stopping for stray passengers and water for the engine. Beyond that, I had never gone down the tracks with the train into unknown territory. My pilgrimage began at the nearest town. My brother, home from university, briefed me on the fine points of train travel and gave me a sleeping pill so I could sleep sitting upright on the wicker seats. The whistle blew, I waved to my brother and left with fear and trembling. A short time later we passed through our village and the tears hit me full force. So many memories flashed through my mind — life on the farm — the schoolhouse — the church my father built — the people I knew — the familiarity of it all. The full impact of what I was leaving behind struck me with no compensating awareness of what was lying in store for me. I sat up all night anxiety stricken about what would happen when I arrived in the city.

My parents had good friends who had agreed to care for me until my parents' arrival. I wore some distinctive clothing, which identified me on arrival, and fortunately, we connected. Then the big world opened up. Street and traffic lights, buses, streetcars, a ride over a big bridge with smoking trains underneath. Exciting but overwhelming. We arrived at 696 College Ave, an address that I remember when over the years I have forgotten the addresses of our many homes. On arrival, I was introduced to running water

and an indoor toilet which I was scared to flush. This replaced our familiar outdoor John. I was tucked into bed and all went well until I heard a train in the distance. Overcome with homesickness, the tears flowed! This is a vivid memory that has remained with me over fifty years. No one can describe the overwhelming feeling of homesickness! It is something that must be experienced to be meaningful. Once tasted, a sensitivity develops toward others in similar situations, which stays with you for life.

Recapturing the feelings experienced in an earlier stage of life is very difficult, especially if these were very moving episodes. Adjusting to city life was such an event. Around every corner there was the unknown. What I thought would be exciting in essence became a threat — a new experience requiring skills I simply didn't possess. I didn't know how to use a phone, ride a bus, pay the fare, ask and use a transfer or know where to get off the bus. I had never been on a streetcar, rode an elevator or escalator, just to mention a few impediments.

The people I was staying with were unaware of the depth of my unfamiliarity. I have often thought about the appropriateness of the old saying which they should have adopted — assume ignorance and proceed from there. They assumed I possessed the knowledge and understanding of a typical city seventeen year old — an incorrect assumption. Feeling very insecure and trying to preserve my faltering image, I tried to bluff it through, often with embarrassing results. Thinking about this, I was reminded of Orphan Annie and her dog Sandy walking down the streets of New York and Annie saying to her dog "No where can you be so alone as in a big city."

The moving finger writes; and having writ,
Moves on: nor all thy Piety nor Wit
Shall lure it back to cancel half a Line,
Nor all thy Tears wash out a word of it.
Omar Khayyam

Chapter Nine
The Farm Boy and the City School

Memories of my first school day will always stay with me and call forth feelings of discomfort. Just reflecting on this day is unpleasant. While today I can now sit back and view the occasion impartially, I still feel sad for the boy who was so overcome by it all! The day began with the challenge of getting to school on my own. My hostess had to leave for work very early. Prior to leaving, she told me where I should go to catch the bus, to buy five tickets for a quarter and use one for the trip. However I didn't know that I was to stand at the bus stop across the street to catch the bus. As a result, I missed the first bus and became very anxious wondering if another would be along in time. Finally, it arrived. I mounted the steps got my ticket but didn't know what to do with it. I handed it to the driver who abruptly, to my embarrassment, told me to put it in the box. I felt everyone was watching and my discomfort went sky high.

I had the address where I was to get off but, being unfamiliar with the preceding streets, passed the location and had a long walk back. Eventually I arrived at the school but I was late. The forty-room school, compared to my previous one and two room schools, was overwhelming. It was orientation day but I didn't know where to go and was too shy to

ask. I discovered after the fact, that students were first assembled in the gym to receive information on activities of that day and the year to come. Having missed the session, I was at a loss what to do and spent most of the day wandering around avoiding conversation with other students. Finally, a teacher observing my confusion took me to what was to become my homeroom. Arriving late, attention was focused on me, which increased my anxiety. This was compounded by the teacher asking me how to spell my name. I felt all eyes were focused on this odd ball with a strange foreign name. All I wanted was to disappear into a hole in the floor. Shortly thereafter, the day mercifully came to an end. I hastily left, looking straight ahead, walked as fast as I could without attracting attention, caught the bus and returned home. I cannot remember that evening's conversation. I do, however, recall going to bed as soon as possible and crying myself to sleep.

> *What's in a name! That which we call a rose*
> *by any other name would smell as sweet.*
> *William Shakespeare*

The next day was an improvement since I got to the school without difficulty and on time. The first activity involved program registration since I had failed to complete this the preceding day. Once again, I blundered in ignorance. There were two choices: The matriculation route or the general route. Not knowing the difference and not wishing to appear stupid, I chose the general program. A week later I discovered this choice did not provide the courses needed to gain entry to university. To make a change required a referral to a counsellor — another unknown. The learned doctor whose name I still remember, lived up to my fearful expectations. My lack of sophistication obviously did not impress him. Reviewing my brief and unimpressive history, his wise advice was for me to go back to the farm — a demoralizing comment. Somehow I pulled myself together sufficiently to challenge his insensitive guidance. The result was a change in program accompanied with the prediction of certain failure. One so often forgets what a lifelong impact an authority figure can have on a child. Clearly, the counsellor was an unhappy man who vented his hostility against a defenseless non-threatening person —a common human reaction.

Shortly thereafter, I found myself in a grade ten Math class, the only boy there. Looking around at the well-dressed classmates, my farm boy attire stood out. I felt and probably acted like a hick. But the situation worsened! The teacher, an old maid I later discovered, obviously was displeased by my intrusion into her all girl class. My complete innocence made little difference. She seemed to vent her animosity by having me go to the black board to solve a Math problem that was completely over my head. She let me stand there for what seemed an eternity and then allowed me, red faced and totally humiliated, to return to my seat. One fringe benefit: as the year wore on I developed a comfort level with girls.

We fear things in proportion to our ignorance of them.
Titus Livy

These early school experiences led me to conclude city life was not for me. I sat down and poured out my unhappiness in a letter to my parents. In it I begged them to allow me to return home to the farm. I promised I would do whatever was expected of me as long as I could return — a natural reaction of a very unhappy boy. The fact that my parents would no longer be living there did not cross my mind. Fortunately, for me the dye was cast — there was no turning back. My parents' arrival made all the difference. I had a home base where I could lick my wounds — a place where I was accepted without reservation. Operating from a base of security made the world more acceptable.

The neighbours two doors down adopted me as their surrogate son. Their only child, a daughter my age, included me in her group of friends. I quickly became involved in their activities which included Sunday evening sing-a-longs and treats hosted by the neighbours. This, amazingly, they did week after week. I soon called them Mom and Pop. They were quite a contrast to my elderly parents whose Germanic background and accents set them apart and, I regret to say, at my age made them less appealing in my eyes. A nearby neighbour, a very successful bachelor and an accomplished pianist, also took an interest in me and exposed me to the thrills of piano music. To this day when I hear Chopin's Polonaise I think back fondly on George. Good fortune, the Hand of God, so often enters one's life when it is needed most.

Gradually I developed a comfort level at school but I was still handicapped by a lack of social skills, which reduced self-confidence. I was strong and athletically fit after a summer of hard physical farm work. I often stood at the sidelines of the sports field watching the football practice. Many of the players looked whimpy to me and I believed did not possess my physical prowess. I wanted to try out for the team, the school's elite, but was reluctant to do so since I knew nothing about football. Better not to try than to do so and display one's ignorance. By not venturing, I could always play the, I could have if I had wanted to, game. Who could challenge that!

Franz Schubert commented that "Some people come into our lives, leave footprints on our hearts, and we are never the same." My homeroom teacher was such a man. He seemed to understand my adjustment challenges and went out of his way to help pave the way. One day when the class was misbehaving, as punishment, the teacher gave the group an additional assignment to be handed in the next day. At day's end, as the class was leaving, he asked me to stay behind. Immediately I thought of a host of possible misdemeanors I must have committed. To my surprise he said that he appreciated how well behaved I was in class and I was to disregard the class assignment but keep it to myself. That day I left the classroom walking ten feet off the ground — a tremendous boost to my self-image. I began to think that I wasn't that deficient after all. It takes so little to make a difference.

Gradually grade ten came to an end. My first year was pre-occupied with gaining social acceptance at all costs and my grades reflected this — a bare pass in most subjects. I was, however, beginning to feel better about myself. In fact, I felt proud about attending a big time school. Furthermore, I had friends who readily accepted me and city life gradually became more appealing. What a difference a year makes!

I still looked forward with great anticipation to returning to my former farm community with my parents to work on my brother's farm during the summer. There I soon displayed a patronizing attitude towards my former public school classmates. I had become a city slicker and they were still country bumpkins. Big time, put down, behaviour, built on a base of inadequacy, is such a common human frailty and I played it to the hilt. How quickly I had forgotten the feelings of inferiority I experienced when first confronted with what I felt was a sophisticated urban environment. Gradually, as I developed insight, I discovered unrecognized skills and learned to cope with my feelings of inadequacy, I began to accept myself for what I was. It took time to realize that developing my natural abilities and personality was the best strategy. Besides, it provided the means of ringing true as a person — the beginnings of real growth! The disciple Timothy so aptly emphasized this when he said, "Neglect not the gift that is in thee." (1 Timothy 4:4)

The summer soon came to an end and I returned to the city with considerable enthusiasm. What a marked contrast to my first entry one year earlier! I felt like Joshua entering Jericho after the walls collapsed. The school year saw a modest improvement in my grades and a gradual expansion of friendships. Feeling I was one of the crowd made such a difference. A part time job delivering groceries on my bike allowed me to buy a few window dressing items. These, to me, more firmly secured my acceptance as a group member, a high priority. I was still struggling with feelings of being an unsophisticated farm boy of ethnic background. Gradually I developed sufficient confidence to attend Friday night teen dances where I learned to do the "Dip" and developed enough confidence to walk a girl home after the dance. That was real living! When the term was over I again returned to my brother's farm with my parents. The fall saw me returning for my final high school year. Although the year was not marked by academic success, it was socially rewarding. Friends encouraged me to try out for the Gilbert and Sullivan Mikado operetta. I suppose my previous training singing "You Are My Sunshine" to cows at milking time, helped refine my singing voice and gave me the courage to try out for the chorus. Much to my amazement and joy, I was accepted. Being matched with a delightfully charming singing partner, who became a very good friend, provided the icing on the cake. Performing on the stage of the city's main theatre almost compared favourably with the master of ceremonies performance at my grade school Christmas concert. In my own mind I had arrived — another confidence building milestone.

I completed high school with a less than impressive academic record — just barely adequate to eventually gain entry to university. Graduation exercises should stand out in my mind as a high point but that was not the case. My parents felt very close to me and, wishing to share the moment, attended the graduation ceremonies. To this day, I still feel ashamed to admit that I would have preferred they had not attended. Being old, and obviously foreign, was an embarrassment to me. The perceptions of my classmates and teachers were my main concern. I had come a long way in my personal development, but my insecurity was still my over-riding preoccupation. William Shakespeare put this into perspective with his comment, "What errors drive our eyes and ears amiss."

So many times in life one would like to achieve redemption for past behaviour or feelings. I wish I could do this with my parents — to make amends — to say I'm sorry! The best I can do is understand why I felt as I did and perhaps help others to cope with similar feelings. Many have commented that the hardest person to forgive is yourself. That's where it must start if real healing is to take place. But memory lingers on! Being freed up to talk about it helps remove the burden of guilt. George Bernard Shaw's evaluation has been a source of comfort to me. He wrote, "The more things a man is ashamed of, the more respectable he is."

I always intended going on to university but to do so I had to earn money. My retired parents, living on a very modest income, were not in a position to help me. On completing high school I got a job working at a cheese factory earning the heady sum of fifty cents an hour. After paying my parents for my board and room, and being somewhat careless with my earnings, little money remained for higher education. Consequently, I decided to stay on at the factory. My diligence was rewarded with a promotion to the second floor where I was given sole responsibility for making mincemeat. This early exposure to trust whetted my appetite for similar experiences. The factory was a roughhouse, earthy place where my unworldliness soon became apparent. Older married women took great delight in telling me dirty stories causing me to blush and producing howls of laughter. The working world was not what I thought it would be! At day's end, I took the bus home carrying the strong factory cheese smells with me. Those riding with me did not give me admiring glances!

Success is just one long street fight.

Milton Berle

Eventually, I decided to look for work in a cleaner smelling place. This led me to respond to an ad describing the glowing pleasures flowing from employment as a bank teller. When I was interviewed in my finest clothes, free of factory smells, I convincingly described my lifelong desire to work in a bank. To my surprise, I was hired for a princely salary of sixty dollars a month. This was less than I was making at the factory but provided considerably more status. I still remember the uplifting feeling associated with standing behind the bank counter. I was rubbing elbows with the money boys! My parents were equally impressed. After a period of orientation I was given my booth and a money till to go with it. The anxiety associated with responsibility for gobs of money was enhanced by the presence of a loaded revolver in the back of the till. Bank insurance apparently required such a weapon. The accountant, however, firmly warned me never to use it regardless of what happened. Actually, with my gopher shooting experience on the farm, I would have been a good shot. However, I had enough sense not to mention this.

If I ever had second thoughts about a career in banking, a year's exposure quickly changed my mind. In those days all transactions were manually recorded on what was referred to as a blotter. Approaching three p.m. I had already tallied up the day's take only amending the listing with last minute transactions. As soon as the accounts were balanced I put up my hand to have the accountant check me out. When this was done, I left for the day without looking for ways to increase my knowledge of banking — something my seniors noticed. As the time for starting university approached, I considered ways of leaving that would still keep my reputation intact. I sought the advice of the accountant as to whether I should consider a career in banking or go on to university. Much to my relief, the accountant expressed the viewpoint that I was more suited to being a scholar than a banker — a sweeping assumption. With this I heartily agreed and left on a high note. I must say that all was not lost. In later years, when I became an academic administrator, my banking experience was of considerable help in budgeting. Varied life events should never be under-valued!

When people say it's not the money — it's the money.
Toronto Globe and Mail

Chapter Ten
Entering the Halls of Learning

My reasons for pursuing a university education were, at best, poorly defined. I saw it as the key to success. Like so many young people I hadn't really thought it through. Somehow, I believed that entering university would open the window to great insight and fulfillment — the grand misconception. When the bells didn't ring and the lights didn't blaze, I was quite disillusioned. It didn't matter that my expectations were unrealistic in the first place.

Looking back, various factors influenced my decision to attend university. The feeling of elevation that accompanied my decision to go on to high school still percolated in the back of my mind. I might not have wanted to admit that going on to university greatly enhanced my self-image, but to me it did. Just carrying a briefcase full of books was elevating and I hoped everyone on the bus took notice. Even the people at the cheese factory and to some extent, my former bank co-workers raised their hats to me. I must be smart and I needed that reinforcement. I was still that little orphan boy with all the accompanying hang-ups. I had made progress in confidence building but I still had to prove I had more going for me than people realized, even though it mattered little to others. I was driven in the same way as the millionaire, who having acquired his first million, has to press on. It was a way of lifting myself up by my bootstraps. People who were educated, escaped their past, I thought. In all fairness to recognize the flaw in such reasoning, at that age, is a bit unrealistic. Such unconscious drives do influence decision-making, which we cloak under the pretense of logic.

Human behaviour is very complex. No one occurrence determines what we do. In my case, role model influence played a major role. An older brother, who had completed a Science degree and later entered Medicine, became the one I erroneously attempted to emulate even though his skills and aptitudes varied markedly from mine. With little, if any curriculum research, I enrolled in Science. The program included courses such as Physics, Chemistry and Biology for which I was ill prepared and for which I had little natural ability or interest. The results were not surprising. I hated the courses and my marks undoubtedly placed me within the bottom ten percent of the class. Worse still, was the impact this had on my self-evaluation. It reluctantly led me to question my ability to succeed at university. Perhaps I had simply been deluding myself? Certainly comparing my performance to that of my talented brother left much to be desired. I began to wonder if the dreams I had nurtured were simply dreams! The term ended with me being disillusioned. I was so embarrassed that I told no one of my scholastic record. I simply said the year went well.

Worse still, I had almost run out of money. My parents had no source of income other than my father's meagre old age pension and the bit of money from the sale of their farm. Consequently, in addition to paying my tuition, I also paid my parents room and board. I was at a crisis point in my life. Following in my brother's footsteps simply hadn't worked. A different strategy was needed. I hadn't planned ahead. Noah started building long before it started raining.

With the end of the term came the need to earn some money.

Fortunately, I quickly got a job delivering ice. The man interviewing me, evaluating my size questioned my ability to carry up to fifty pounds of ice on my back. Somehow, reassuring him I was a farm boy used to hard work, convinced him to give me a try. Besides, I had the necessary driver's licence. Hoping to impress my boss, I did the route faster than expected. Rather than being complimented for my diligence, I was relieved of the truck and given a horse, which better fit the time schedule. This was my first introduction to questionable management practices. But the job had fringe financial benefits. Customers, who appreciated my services or simply felt sorry for me, placed notes on the icebox encouraging me to take a beer. I hadn't as yet acquired a taste for beer, that came later. Not wishing to be unappreciative or miss a financial opportunity, I cooled the ill-gotten gains in the back of my ice wagon. The more seasoned co-workers soon became aware of this treasure trove and were only too glad to compensate me at the going rate. My arrival at the end of the day was heralded with cheers of "Here comes the kid!" Little did I know I was in Al Capone's league as a bootlegger! It's amazing the benefits that flow from a university education!

During the summer, I made friends with someone attending United College, a small United Church funded institution in Winnipeg. They spoke glowingly of the place and encouraged me to consider enrolling there. Based on this non-professional counselling, I decided to do so. In applying, I concealed my blotchy year in Science at the University of Manitoba and my high school grades were adequate to gain acceptance. Reviewing potential programs of study with the Registrar/Counsellor, I was encouraged to enrol in Arts, which included courses such as Psychology, Sociology, Philosophy, etc, which seemed fascinating. To my surprise and delight I enjoyed them immensely. Amazingly also, I achieved top marks. How could this be? My poor performance in Science had left an indelible imprint on me. I couldn't accept the possibility I might have something going for me. Perhaps the College was a second class institution or professors simply felt sorry for me. Gradually, as the term progressed, I reluctantly accepted my new-found standing hoping no one would discover otherwise. Paul Sweeney's evaluation that, "True success is overcoming the fear of being unsuccessful," aptly described my state of mind.

I financed my first year selling suits at The Bay and at Tip Top Tailors two nights a week. I also worked as a Counsellor at a local church applying my psychological skills as I learned them.

Professor Cliff, my United College psychology instructor, entered my life when I needed the support of someone whom I greatly respected. Cliff was such a man. He took a liking to me and judged me competent to mark multiple choice exams for him. That this learned professor saw fit to take me under his wing was very uplifting. Cliff, appreciating my financial problems, recommended me for a part-time position at a school for boys who were wards of the state. The job included supervising homework, running the gym, readying kids for bed and overseeing the dorm as well as providing support and superficial counselling. Cliff's recommendation carried considerable weight with the director who expressed concerns regarding my youthfulness and lack of experience. With a false sense of bravado, I assured him I could do the job well. No doubt Cliff's recommendation saved the day. His on-going support and advice made survival possible — the difference between success and failure. The position provided room and board, laundry facilities, meals, plus a sixty-dollar a month salary in exchange for a forty-hour workweek. In 1950 this was a fair salary that kept me self sufficient at university. The income couldn't have come at a better time.

The position opened my eyes to child neglect and suffering and was a tremendous practicum supplementing what I learned in the classroom. Some sixty kids ranging in age from nine to sixteen were housed in comfortable dorms and were well fed and clothed. All had come from dysfunctional families, many had been abused, improperly fed and some had simply been abandoned and, consequently, had become wards of the State. All suffered from emotional neglect, few had developed adequate life skills and all hungered for love and attention. Addressing these needs as a young man in my 20's was an overwhelming challenge. Even the little I did in terms of establishing relationships seemed to bear fruit.

Every group includes unique characters. One in particular stands out. A young boy had just been brought back by the police for attempting to pilfer money from a Safeway store. His return coincided with a ladies annual speech-giving event where children competed for prizes awarded for speaking on a topic of their choice. This delightfully charming but manipulative child got up, and without preparation, spoke about "The Bible story I love the best." I was seated beside one of the judges who being enthralled by the performance said, "Isn't he an angel?" Little did she know! She agreed with the others to award him first prize. I often wonder if he ever put his talents to constructive use. One never knows what may happen. Years later I encountered one of the more troublesome graduates of the school at a church. Familiar with his past behaviour and bracing myself for the worst, I was pleasantly surprised to discover he was married, had a good job, taught Sunday school, and also treated me with affection.

The episode that put things into perspective for me was the last breakfast I had at the school. I had been there for three years during the winters and was now leaving to go to army camp to complete my training as an officer cadet. Thereafter, I planned to look for full time employment hopefully in a psychological field. I remember so well reading the 91st psalm at the breakfast assembly — something we did daily. When breakfast was over, a boy, probably age nine or thereabouts, came up to me and extended his folded fist to give me something. He said, "I was going to get you a going away present but I couldn't get to the store. Here is 68 cents. Buy yourself a going away present." I was choked up with emotion as I thanked and hugged him for his generosity. It reminded me of the widow's mite who gave all she had — so did he. I am still overwhelmed by this generous act, a high point in my life. I wish I had preserved that 68 cents in a frame.

Often I have reflected on this episode. It made me appreciate that it isn't always the big deal items in life that make a big difference. It also made me realize that I may have underestimated the impact I had. It took a small child to put things into perspective. I was truly grateful that I had the opportunity to experience this environment. It made an indelible impression on me. The whole experience made me so aware that it takes little to enrich the life of a child who accepts what you do without judgement. The exposure helped me to grow and resulted in a positive re-evaluation of myself. Once again it was a series of small events that enhanced my development.

During my first year at college I developed what I thought was a true friendship with a chap from Trinidad. He told me captivating tales about his influential father, which subsequently proved to be pure fabrication. I was charmed by his glibness and felt privileged to have him as a friend. When he told me that his father's cheque for tuition was lost in the mail and he was in danger of being kicked out of college, I unhesitatingly believed him. Helping him out of his dilemma, I lent him a hundred dollars, a third of my summer's earnings. In due course I discovered he was doing the town on my money — a hard-learned lesson.

A fool and his money were lucky to get together in the first place.
Night Court's Harry Anderson

A big problem was the lack of study time. I survived by taking off several weeks before exams and focused on memorizing the year's work. This strategy earned me passing grades but ensured little retention of what I had memorized; a problem when I later tried to gain entry into postgraduate schools. So many times in life one is faced with the choice of doing something poorly or doing nothing at all. Moving in the right direction, even in a wobbly fashion, seemed to have definite advantages. Abraham Lincoln when questioned about the value of spending endless hours on studies that didn't seem to lead anywhere commented, "I will study and get ready and maybe my chance will come."

Chapter Eleven
The Military

During World War II, I was walking with my brother, an army captain, when he was saluted by a soldier. I was most impressed and well remember thinking how nice it would be for me to receive such recognition. The need to be noticed, to stand apart from the crowd, to be seen as a person of consequence and worth is a very powerful motivating force, especially for one handicapped by feelings of inadequacy.

During my early years at university, I became aware of the military's interest in attracting men having officer potential. The Canadian Officer Training Corp (COTC) was designed for this purpose. What led me to conclude I possessed leadership ability, I do not know. Dreams surpassed critical evaluation. Those accepted took classes one night a week and attended a three-year summer training program at a military camp. I inquired and was encouraged to apply. Upon successful completion of the entrance requirements I was asked to choose the branch I would like to enter: Artillery, Infantry or the Armoured (tank) Corp. Knowing little about any and being obliged to decide, I selected the Armoured Corps since I believed this branch involved less walking. I already had my fill of walking behind the horse drawn harrows on the farm. For once I lucked out! Perhaps I was influenced by the Chinese proverb "He who deliberates fully before taking a step will spend his entire life on one leg."

Basic training included lengthy route marches, outdoor camping and endless hours of drill. Each cadet took his turn in front of the platoon directing the marching. This I enjoyed. My experience as master of ceremonies at my public school concert provided the needed foundation training. With my exposure to rugged farm work, I found army training a piece of cake. Besides, the pay was better than any other summer job and included good board, room, clothing, and led somewhere.

Evenings focused on getting one's kit ready for the next day but included considerable spare time. Cadets routinely were obliged to get haircuts with an emphasis on shortness not fashion. I decided to take advantage of this need and set up a barbershop charging twenty-five cents a cut. There was the added benefit that this became the social centre for the dorm and I was part of it. Another cadet seeing the financial benefits I was receiving, decided to go into competition. He, however, lacked the prerequisite skills. His first, and only effort, proved disastrous. Not knowing where to start he had his victim put on his beret and cut the hair close to the skin stopping at the bottom of the hat. The unveiling revealed what looked like a toadstool. Filled with fear of what the inspecting sergeant would say, the casualty came to me for a remedy. The only solution was a brush cut, for which I charged an additional 25 cent punitive fee.

Cadets were also expected to do their own laundry and iron their uniforms to inspection perfection. There were a few momma's boys in the group who lacked the skills or interest to do this on their own. Once again, I saw this as a potential business opportunity and contracted to do laundry and ironing at a price. My hearty background provided the foundation skills and motivation. Coming from the wrong side of the tracks was not an impediment but an advantage. This allowed me to bank my entire salary as well as enjoy life at the mess on my earnings. Additionally,

I earned the respect and acceptance of my peers who put on a birthday celebration for me — the barber. The benefits of taking advantage of an opportunity are reflected in the following story:

> *A mouse was taking her children for a walk across the kitchen floor. A*
> *cat appeared. The mouse looked at the cat and began to bark like a*
> *dog. The cat ran away, whereupon the mouse turned to her children*
> *and said, "See it always helps to know a second language."*
>
> *Dave Osborn*

Years later, as a college dean, I wondered why more students didn't supplement their income by performing mundane tasks, rather than becoming excessively burdened with student loans. I couldn't help questioning if their generation had been robbed of the opportunity and the initiative needed for entrepreneurial skill development. Perhaps their overly protective and indulgent parents inadvertently developed crippling attitudes, expectations and appetites. In so doing, they robbed their children of necessary growth opportunities. Parental training and personal experience taught me tremendous satisfaction can be realized through self-sufficiency.

Three summers were spent acquiring skills in gunnery, tactics, map reading, tank manoeuvring and maintenance. Learning the principles of war and leadership as a platoon leader were foundation skills that proved to be very helpful throughout my various careers. Training in how to act as an officer and gentleman helped offset my unsophisticated background and was decidedly beneficial. This included a mess dinner using all the fancy dishes, cutlery and wineglasses. My farm background had only exposed me to a knife, fork and spoon. Anything more than that was an intimidating mystery. We were given a detailed course in etiquette, the purpose and use of each utensil, the passing of the port, and the appropriate way of excusing yourself, if it was vital that you leave the table. This exposure helped prepare me for many varied dining functions.

The day of graduation came with much pomp and circumstance. Marches, preceded by hours of rehearsal, were accompanied by a brass band that made one's hair stand up in the back of the neck. The final act was the inspection by the Commandant walking between the rows of cadets accompanied by his two Scotty dogs. As he was coming around the corner of the row in front of me, one of his dogs lifted his leg and peed on the pants of a cadet who remained ram rod stiff at attention — a true military officer. I remember thinking, "A soldier's last farewell." The awarding of a second lieutenant commissioning scroll made it all worth while and I felt good about myself and the accomplishments I had achieved. In due course I was promoted to Lieutenant.

As a young officer I thought up schemes that provided means of escaping extended mess dinners which frequently embraced purely superficial masculine officer events. These included acts of physical prowess such as arm wrestling, consuming a yard of beer without stopping to take a breath, poker games where you were expected to lose to those senior to you, listening to military accomplishments embroidered over time. The unwritten rule was that you were obliged to remain until the most senior officer present left. This often extended into the wee hours with behaviour becoming progressively less appealing. As I was researching the premises, I discovered a door next to the downstairs toilet exiting directly to a sheltered driveway. This proved to be my escape route. I worked out a clandestine plan that worked perfectly. At an agreed to time, when several hours of hilarious activity had elapsed, I made a point of walking around, talking to people, ensuring I was noticed. Having done so, I made my way to the downstairs toilet, checked to see no one was around, dashed out the side door to a waiting car and roared off. While the less fortunate were still confined to the mess for hours, I was long snoozing in bed. The next day some people commented that they hadn't seen much of me but accepted the statement that I was caught up in a poker game. Devious but effective!

As a young lieutenant my naivete led me to the faulty assumption that all officers were gentlemen. I subsequently discovered this was a gross exaggeration. Many, hiding behind their rank, displayed behaviour to the contrary. Some very senior officers at fancy social events, prior to harassment legislation, pinched wives' bottoms because they got away with it. Officers junior to them, and their wives, often tolerated such abuse since they feared career ramifications. Fortunately, such extreme behaviour was uncommon. In all fairness, such conduct is not confined to the military! I later realized abusive, bullying behaviour of an insecure person, regardless of where it occurs is demeaning, generates hostility and is certainly demotivating. Often, the loss of capable employees is the end result. Self-respect is important! Class has not gone out of style!

> *Culture is one thing and varnish another.*
> *Ralph Waldo Emerson*

Shortly after earning my commission I married the love of my life. I met Selma (Sel) at a university function in Winnipeg. She wore a green plaid suit and was strikingly pretty. When the event concluded, someone offered me a ride. To my delight I discovered Sel was also included and, more surprisingly, lived on my street. With tactful prompting I was invited in to tea. I discovered she and her roommates were all Trans Canada Airline stewardesses and nurses, an airline qualification requirement at that time. To say I wasn't enamoured is an understatement. Air travel was in its infancy and by no means commonplace. For someone who had never been in a plane, knowing a stewardess was boastworthy. Sel's picture accompanied me through officer's training and was the subject of much admiration and wonder about what she saw in me.

Sel grew up on a farm in Northern Alberta with five brothers. When we decided to marry, it seemed appropriate that the only daughter return home to the farm for the event. Airline policy required stewardesses to resign when they married, but Sel was given a free ride back to Edmonton as a parting gift. I left Toronto to join her at her home, driving a used car bought by pooling our resources. Along the way I stopped in Winnipeg to pick up my father. My mother's poor health required her to fly to Grande Prairie to join us.

Car problems necessitated a stop in Edmonton where I phoned Sel's brother, the first contact I had made with a family member. He came out to the garage to scrutinize the interloper. I am a small man and Sel's brothers are all over six feet. Later I heard that when her brother was queried about this Paul guy he put things in perspective with the comment, "He's not a bad little guy but if there ever is a fight I'll put my money on Selma."

We continued on back woods roads since the paved highway from Edmonton to Grande Prairie had not been built. My father, a man of few words after a particularly rough and dusty section commented, "You are like a prince charming going into the wilderness to rescue your bride." Eventually, negotiating ruts and mud holes we got within a mile of the farm-site only to become completely mired in gumbo.

My father and I walked the last mile to the farm and the hand built log house. Not having previously met the parents, it was a challenging moment! Fortunately, Sel's father was a small man and we saw eye to eye.

The wedding was to take place in the local small country church. The floor was made of boards and hand-hewn pews provided seating. Several days before the event, Sel and I did a thorough dusting in readiness for the big event. The marriage ceremony was performed by the local family pastor using the text from Matthew 6:33, "Seek ye first the kingdom of God and all things will be given unto you." Music was provided by a family member playing a foot-pumper organ. The reception took place in the family farmhouse followed by dancing in the yard. Sel's dad played the accordion and a neighbour accompanied him on the violin. Both were accomplished European musicians and misplaced home-steaders. Since that date, three daughters, a son and nine grand children continue to brighten our lives.

Chapter Twelve
A Family Development

While I was undergoing officer cadet training, I received a letter from my father informing me that one of my non-adopted, birth brothers had contacted Child Welfare wishing to make contact with me. My father wrote asking what action I wished to take. I responded saying I had no desire to pursue this. I emphasized the point that, for me, my mother and father were my real parents and my adopted family was my only family and I desired no other. I felt very strongly that to do otherwise would be an insult to my parents and my family who had shown such unreserved love for me. I was proud to be a family member; I had adopted their heritage as my own and did not wish anything to impact on the relationship that I enjoyed. Interestingly, my parents never mentioned this again, nor did I. Somehow there did not seem to be a need for discussion. The chapter had been closed.

Frequently one reads accounts of adopted children becoming unduly preoccupied with attempts to discover their roots. While I can understand the logic for doing so, I am also convinced this is a non-productive activity with lasting negative results. More times than not the discovery leads to heartache. The romantic image that has been nurtured over time proves faulty. Additionally, there exists the danger that such pursuits will adversely influence existing family relationships. The feeling of familial unworthiness develops which is difficult to erase. Those who choose this route fail to realize that it takes more than being related to have something in common. At some point you must decide where you belong.

I never made a big deal about being adopted nor did I mention it to my children when they were small. I wished to prevent such knowledge impairing the warm relationships they were developing with my adopted family. My oldest daughter, inadvertently, through an old friend of my mother's, became aware that I was adopted. When my daughter asked me about this I quite openly told her what I knew. Interestingly and surprisingly, she inquired if Mother knew and was comforted to discover this was the case. In due course, as events unfolded, all four children were informed with a minimum of fanfare. A positive result was that my children developed as close a relationship with my family as I enjoyed.

Years later, at my children's urging, I contacted child welfare for any historical information on my file which I shared with my children. I also had a family discussion centred around the question of whether they wished me to explore contacts with my natural family members. This could only be done if I instigated it. All the children, but one, expressed no desire in doing so. In depth, discussion led to the conclusion that curiosity was the only reason why one of the children wished to pursue the matter further. When it became apparent that any contact obligated an ongoing relationship, the issue was dropped. The only real benefit I could see in pursuing the family tree would be medical information. Since I am a senior and uncommonly healthy, this was not considered a justifiable reason for opening relationships.

> *You can't change your ancestors but you can do*
> *something about your descendants.*
>
> Wes Izzard

Chapter Thirteen
Back to the Military

During my officer cadet training I became aware that the army had a personnel selection branch which included the kind of work that appealed to me. I also discovered that there was a personnel office on the base. Wishing more information, I asked for an appointment with the major who headed up the unit. The major, for whatever reason, took a liking to me. Since I had three weeks left in my training, he arranged to have me assigned to the personnel office where two experienced officers took me under their wing and treated me as a seasoned personnel officer. They became lifelong friends. These men allowed me to do most of the usual interviews coming into the office, ranging from disciplinary problems to personnel applying to be commissioned from the ranks. I had advanced from being an officer cadet to an officer — a great confidence builder. The prestige of the office, by association, also enhanced my self-esteem. One day the application of a corporal, who previously had singled me out for special abuse on the parade square, appeared on my desk. He was applying to be considered for commissioning as an officer. Needless to say, I could not deal with his application. I was, however, struck by the irony of it all. It reminded me of the old saying: What goes around comes around.

My short exposure to the work convinced me that this was what I would love to do as a career. The major, sensing my interest, pulled strings to have me stay on with the hope that a spot might be found for me. In due course, a temporary position became available at a personnel depot in Toronto interviewing candidates for the military. I loved the work, which allowed me to put the psychological training that I had to work. Unfortunately, the commanding officer saw me as a pip-squeak with little aptitude. This became apparent when on different occasions I sent two applicants to him with the recommendation that they not be accepted. He showed his disdain for my advice by writing a directive across my recommendation that they be enrolled. Not a sign of endorsement! Since I had no choice, I did so.

However, I included reasons why I believed the applicants were considered unsuitable but were being enrolled at the direction of the commanding officer — a not too tactful action especially in a military setting. Nevertheless, I was convinced I was right and was prepared to stand by my decision. I also believed my personal reputation was at risk and had to be defended.

A reputation once broken may possibly be repaired but the world always keeps its eye on the spot where the crack is.
Detroit News

I was exceedingly lucky! In due course, both men were released as unsuitable; one for theft, the other for mental instability. Furthermore, the commanding officer was obliged to explain why he had ignored the good advice of his personnel officer. This infuriated him.

Shortly thereafter, a serviceman, who was entitled to a military funeral, died at a nearby hospital. I was called in by the commandant and told that I was in charge of funeral arrangements despite my objection that I had never done this. Clearly my failure was hoped for! In desperation, I phoned my old personnel officer friend at my previous camp who took on the defense of a confrere as a challenge. In due course, he phoned to tell me that he had arranged for a demonstration ceremonial platoon to meet me at the funeral site. Being very aware of my ineptness, he strongly encouraged me to simply meet the sergeant major, return his salute, ask him to carry on and get out of the way. This I did with considerable relief. The town had never experienced such a dramatic performance. The parents wished to express their gratitude, in an official way, even though I assured them this was unnecessary. At their persistence, and taking advantage of the moment, I gave them the name and address of the Commanding General. They subsequently wrote him singing my praises. The General in turn wrote my commandant directing him to congratulate me on the General's behalf. This the Commandant did with considerable animosity. The abuse was worth it! I conducted several military funerals that summer but by then I was an expert. In fact it became a challenge to make each funeral more spectacular than the last. The episode reminded me of the comment quoted in Grit, "people usually get what's coming to them — unless it's been mailed."

This incident was the making of me. I became known to the head of Personnel Selection, a full Colonel who decided he wanted me in the organization as a regular officer. While this was going on, I was attempting to gain entry into graduate school since I was still uncertain if I wished to pursue a military career. Having recently married, my focus on life had taken on a new dimension.

All my applications to graduate schools were rejected. One Dean wrote me a demoralizing note saying, that while obtaining a bachelor's degree under very adverse circumstances was commendable, one cannot live down the sins of the past — my poor under-graduate record. I should have known better than think I could achieve a master's degree. Nevertheless, despite rejections, I still felt I had what it took. My self-confidence was gradually being developed — I could not throw in the sponge.

Only he who attempts the ridiculous can achieve the impossible.
Joseph Addison

Fate, or the hand of God, does move in mysterious ways. A professor from the University of British Columbia, a reserve forces personnel officer, came to the personnel depot for an orientation session. Over a beer, I lamented my academic rejections and attempted to present my weak record in the best possible light, emphasizing the fact that I had been obliged to work full time. Ed, after listening to my sad tale of woe, contacted the head of personnel selection who must have given me a favourable rating. To my surprise Ed advised me to reapply. I did so and in a few weeks received notification that I had been accepted for graduate studies with the requirement to do one or two make up courses with Ed serving as my supervisor. Certainly a high point in my life! Again, one person made such a timely impact! Plutarch as early as 46 AD was aware of this when he said, "Even a nod from a person who is esteemed is of more force than a thousand arguments or studied sentences from others." Ed remained a constant source of encouragement until his untimely death.

I decided to let my application for a regular commission stand but with the stipulation that I be posted to Vancouver and be allowed to complete a Master's degree at the University of British Columbia. The chairman of the selection committee, a colonel from the old school, asked me if I wasn't being a bit presumptuous. With misplaced confidence and bravado, I replied that I had a chance for a scholarship at the university, which I would have to give up if I entered the army. To my complete amazement, I was notified that I had been accepted and posted to Vancouver. The moral of the story: "When searching for success and contentment, be clear, realistic, but passionate about what you want and stick with your dreams. Clarity, commitment and tenacity wins the day."

In due course, I was posted to Vancouver with the understanding I would be completing make-up courses at the University of British Columbia. My work as a personnel officer proved to be both challenging and rewarding with many episodes enriching the day. The work in part included being a Sherlock Holmes sleuth ferreting out past behaviour and claims to fame, which set the stage for failure. Some examples: One disproportionately self-confident applicant claimed a high school education, which was not reflected in his conversational skills. When asked to describe the courses he took in grade twelve, he claimed Algebra as one of his successes. When asked to outline what Algebra included, he described it as being literature. Subsequent discussions settled for something less than grade school.

A soldier undergoing recruit training was progressing poorly and was referred for evaluation. Wishing to put my psychological training to use, I administered an intelligence test and asked him to respond to the question what does this saying mean "strike while the iron is hot." The soldier promptly replied, "press your pants while the iron is hot." I knew the military had managed to penetrate!

A final example, a Landed Immigrant from Germany, related a past that didn't check out. When pressed to clarify discrepancies he replied saying, "I don't speak too good English." I immediately switched to German and he fainted. I don't know whether the fear of being found out or my linguistic skills were responsible. His removal by a couple of hefty sergeants terminated the interview. The episode greatly enhanced my reputation as an interrogator. Even incidental events, such as this, influence one's reputation and future development. Stories do circulate and become embroidered.

The work was fascinating, I was doing what I was good at and I looked forward to work with considerable enthusiasm. In due course the military allowed me to attend university full time for a year on full pay and allowances as a Lieutenant. This almost unheard of happening was a great confidence builder. For the first time, the pursuit of knowledge for its own sake was rewarding. Prior to that, education was merely a means to an end — a better job or the means of escaping from my past. The achievement of top grades also helped overcome my feelings of academic incompetence. Despite previous evaluations of unsuitability for graduate school, I had proven them wrong. With accomplishments, one quickly forgets past setbacks! My Masters thesis, on officer evaluation, saved my hide on a later occasion.

A requirement for promotion was the passing of standard promotion exams. To the military, knowledge of tactics and related subjects was considered more important for a personnel officer than training in psychology. The head of my Branch, a former president of the Canadian Psychological Association, had some doubts about this. He, however, believed overcoming this hurdle enhanced a personnel officer's creditability and acceptance by the military. Perhaps so! Not being in charge, I had no other choice but to comply. I had little difficulty learning the Principles of War and greatly enjoyed military history. Integrating tactical maps with the physical terrain was something else. To me it was all farmland. Realizing that exams had to be broad based and theoretical, I focused my learning on how best to read and mark maps applying tactical guidelines. The result was that I passed, and seasoned officers with practical field experience failed. Some of them filed a grievance claiming there was something wrong with the exam since they had failed and somehow, with my lack of practical know how, I had passed. One thing I had learned as a graduate student was how to study for and pass exams. Nevertheless, a promotion to Captain resulted.

People who think they know all the answers
aren't up to date on the questions.
Toronto Globe and Mail

There are times when one questions one's career choice. The autocratic military set me to wonder if that life style really was for me. This came to a head when I was pressured to move my family into vacant army quarters. We had just bought a nice home in a civilian setting and I was not prepared to give that up. Rearing my children in a rank oriented environment was not for me. When I threatened to resign, the heat was turned off.

My year in the academic world had introduced me to a freer lifestyle, which was quite a contrast to the military. The attainment of a Masters degree also opened new avenues for me. These I believed, provided greater opportunity to use my professional training than in the military. I overestimated what I had to offer and I failed to consider that every job has its downside and includes a good portion of mundane tasks. I began to look for the Utopia that cannot be found. My mother had an excellent German expression, literally translated, that spoke to this: When the ox has it good he goes on the ice and breaks his leg. Perhaps, I should have heeded Malcolm S. Forbes advice that, "Too many people overvalue what they are not and undervalue what they are."

I resigned my commission and accepted a position as a counsellor with an alcohol rehabilitation centre. Shortly after my arrival, I began to have second thoughts about this line of work. It seemed to lack the spark I was looking for. To test my concerns, I asked to be put in one of the rehabilitation classes as if I was an alcoholic undergoing treatment. Very quickly I realized I had a problem — a negative attitude towards alcoholics. I experienced a great desire to distance myself from the alcoholic group. I wanted others to know I was not so handicapped. With such a bias, I could never be effective as a counsellor. Realizing this, with hat in hand and eating humble crow, I meekly asked the military to take back the prodigal son. This they benevolently did. I had been slated to fill a research position at Army Headquarters which, during my wanderings, had been filled. Consequently, I was posted to a personnel officer position at an army camp across the country until the research position could be made available in Ottawa. My impetuous act placed an unnecessary burden on my wife who was left alone in Calgary to care for two small children. With more effective, realistic research and honest self-examination, all this could have been avoided.

It was at Camp Gagetown, however, that I had the chance to demonstrate my leadership skills. The depot commander went on leave and I was designated acting commander. One day I received a phone call from a moving company, which was in the process of moving a soldier to a new location. The man in charge stated that he would not proceed with the move unless I guaranteed the contents to be vermin free. This was a new experience for which my training as an officer had not prepared me. But I was the man in charge who had to make a decision. In Harry Truman's words, "the buck stops here." In desperation I phoned the medical officer for advice. He informed me that they had a sergeant on staff who was an expert in this field. With relief I asked to have him sent over.

The sergeant and I worked out a strategy for checking out the premises and the code for informing me when the task was done. We proceeded to the scene of the crime using the excuse that the house had to be inspected before the moving took place. I kept the family occupied in the living room while the sergeant checked out the rest of the house. He finally gave me the signal and we left. Once outside I asked him if there were any vermin. He replied, "No sir, just piss and shit." Not everyone can include such experiences as part of their resume! H. Jackson Brown was so right when he stated, "Every person you meet knows something you don't. Learn from them."

After a year's separation the family made our way to my research appointment at Army Headquarters. Initially, I strongly resisted this posting feeling unsuited for such duties. The Colonel, however, informed me that he considered himself a better judge than I was, and he was right I realized later. I had resisted because of fear and unfamiliarity.

Army headquarters in Ottawa swarmed with senior officers. Captains were a dime a dozen and were banished to high level clerical positions with little responsibility. I had worked hard to become an officer only to become a person of little consequence. I hated what I was doing and in some ways hated myself for being there. Surely, I believed I was worth more than that! Feelings of inadequacy returned. Once again miraculous events provided a lifeline to survival.

Officer cadets were trained at various military establishments across the country. A disproportionate number were failing — a very costly occurrence. A board of senior officers concluded that the high attrition was the result of ineffective evaluation processes. To rectify this, my branch head was directed to remedy the situation. My immediate superior was given the task of developing new effective evaluation systems. Just as he was to commence, a detached retina disabled him. As his immediate subordinate, I was given the task — there being no one else readily available. My seniors, expecting little, crossed their fingers and hoped for the best and so did I. Since I was only a lowly Captain, a sweaty old infantry Major with limited schooling and no relevant training, became the credible team figurehead. I considered this a real put down and greatly resented the implication. To some degree I was comforted by my Colonel's assurance that I was in charge of the study and if the Major in any way interfered, he would be removed. A rather mixed image builder — worthy but unworthy. With this, I went out to slay the dragon.

It is better to deserve honours and not have them
than to have them and not deserve them.
Samuel Clements (Mark Twain)

Perhaps, considering the importance of rank in the military, there was justification for this window dressing. Two instances make this clear. One chief instructor, a Lieutenant Colonel, on meeting me asked, "What the

A Journey Through Inadequacy

hell do you know about leadership? You don't even smell like a soldier."
Being cornered and obliged to reply, I responded that I might not be
familiar with hands-on soldiering but I know a hell of a lot about how
soldiers should be evaluated. He looked at me for a moment, chuckled
and commented, "You little bastard, we're going to get along." I had
passed the test. On another occasion, at the officers' mess, an old Major
was having a drink with the colonel. In a loud voice, spoken so I could
hear him, the Major commented, "Marlborough didn't have the help of
a psychologist and did alright." Clearly he wasn't impressed with what I
was doing and he wanted his senior to know. The Colonel, casting a
glance aside caught my eye and winked. I knew I had won the day.

*The reason many persons don't see things in the right
perspective is that they are always looking for an angle.*
The Mountain Ear

I had an ace in the hole. My Masters thesis in essence provided the
basic information needed. I supplemented this with additional data provided by seasoned officers across Canada to give the study credibility. In
addition, I included findings from other military studies that proved
fruitful. I prepared the report, including suggested evaluation methods,
without the team leader's input. At least he didn't interfere. Nevertheless,
when the report was submitted his name was recorded as the author with
me the assistant. I deeply resented this and felt this was akin to plagiarism. My old feelings of insecurity and great resentment returned and
there was nothing I could do about it. The report was submitted and my
wife and I, and three children went on a lengthy holiday.

The search for a scapegoat is the easiest of all hunting expeditions.
Dwight D. Eisenhower

I assumed nothing more would be heard, but to my amazement, on my return, I discovered the report had been accepted in its entirety. Furthermore, I was assigned responsibility for implementing the system across Canada, a tremendous endorsement which wiped the slate clean. To offset resistance, the Chief of Staff provided me with a copy of a letter he had written all commanders obliging them to comply with my directions — heady stuff. This helped to some degree, but I was still fearful and questioned my ability to pull it off. Perhaps failure lurked around the corner!

Through experimentation, I discovered that different approaches gained acceptance. When I dealt with engineers I relied on the presentation of research data supplemented by statistics. At an infantry school, I focussed on the fact that the training officers themselves had generated the data forming the basis of the evaluation system. I was merely the tabulator of results. Still experiencing resistance, and groping for ways to convince the sceptics, I commented that the results were computer analyzed. "Well, why didn't you say so?" was the reaction, and acceptance was forthcoming. Fortunately, computers then were still in their infancy and their limitations were not broadly known.

Halfway through my briefings I was given an accelerated promotion to the rank of Major, which instantly increased my intelligence and acceptability by those I was orienting. My promotion, however, generated considerable animosity amongst my peers. Some openly displayed their resentment since they felt seniority should have taken precedence. Some openly challenged my authority and had to be dealt with. By this time I had developed sufficient confidence to rise to the challenge.

There still existed considerable resistance to the evaluation methods developed. Training officers felt their turf was being invaded. Worse still, this was being done by a psychologist who could talk smart but had no practical, hands on experience. Such resentment was reflected in sneaky ways during one of my orientation sessions. To exemplify, I had a brother who was an army chaplain at the local command headquarters whom I planned to visit on returning from my briefing. Not knowing his phone number, I asked the officer whom I had been working with for help. He called out to the sergeant, "What is the phone number of the padre at headquarters — some Bohunk name." Once again I reverted to that little orphan boy reacting with great resentment. At least I had grown to the point that I kept my feelings under control. Shortly thereafter, the same officer experiencing difficulty with the assessment process requested my assistance. I responded, "Isn't it amazing when you run into difficulty you call on the Bohunk!" Not a classy response, but understandable. I lashed out because I was offended and resented such unfair treatment. I had forgotten that my expertise was respected by those who really counted, but not accepted by some others. Both instances illustrate how quickly feelings of inadequacy can be rekindled. One would think I should by then have mastered such emotions but it didn't bother me as much anymore. Nevertheless, the tendency to react, is never quite erased but with time reappears with decreasing intensity. Just like some smells take you back to your childhood so also do certain verbal stimuli.

> *No one can make you feel inferior without your consent.*
> *Eleanor Roosevelt*

Resistance by training officers to the new methods being proposed still persisted. With a view to gaining acceptance, I convinced superiors to assemble the doubters at Army Headquarters and invite an outside expert to pronounce his evaluation of what was being proposed. This gentleman, after familiarizing himself with the data, expressed a reluctance to come, stating that I was more of an authority than he was — a very humbling compliment. Nevertheless, he came, blessed what was proposed and resistance vanished. There are various ways of skinning a cat! The old adage, that one has no credibility in one's own land, is so true. Ignoring this fact would be unrealistic. The icing on the cake was being invited to review my work at a NATO conference in Europe. Such recognition did so much for me! The scales in my life were starting to tilt in a positive direction. Feelings of inadequacy were gradually assuming less significance.

The whole research and implementation experience was a high point in my life. I had the chance to test my wings and had survived. I also learned that enduring unfair treatment at times is a necessary requirement for success. In addition, I discovered that there was substance to the statement, "The truth will out," — a hard learned lesson.

With growing self-confidence, I dared to think that pursuing a Ph.D. degree was something I could accomplish. This was a big leap from my rural Manitoba one room school roots. As I reflected on this, I was reminded of the hare and the tortoise story with me as the tortoise. Developing self-sufficiency is a lifelong process. It's amazing what commitment and tenacity leads to. Had I acted on the advice of my high school counsellor, to return to the farm, a doctorate would not have been possible. I realized how important it was for youngsters to have dreams and for others to encourage aspirations.

My director, an impressive role model, endorsed my goal and arranged for me to be posted, as a co-ordinator of research, with the Personnel Applied Research Unit, which had a close university affiliation. He also arranged for me to attend university full time for one year on full pay as a Major. Without this financial assistance, I could not have supported my family. Returning to graduate school was intimidating — similar to what I experienced on entering grade school. All my classmates but one were considerably younger, intelligent and seemed to be on top of the latest psychological developments. I couldn't even ask clever questions. My older classmate decided to throw in the sponge and I hated him for doing so. His departure elevated me to elder statesman with the title of Dad.

I was an example of what can be accomplished with reasonable intelligence because it isn't always the brightest that do well. Often the hunger for success and bulldogged application balances the scales. There were many in my class much smarter than me who did less well and some dropped along the way. The only way I survived was to study long into the night. I knew that I could never slack off since I would never recover. Over Christmas, I only took off Christmas Day and went back to the books. Fortunately I had a breadth of experience which, occasionally, provided an advantage. Failure was out of the question since my entire reputation was at stake. Many were counting on me to do well, especially my family who did without my support as I struggled on. Others, whom I had by-passed on promotion, would have delighted in my failure. Fear of failure can be a great motivator.

The greatest source of inspiration was my wife. She daily saw me disappear into the den shortly after dinner and stay there, long into the night, leaving her to look after the children. While neighbourhood wives had their husbands to share the evening with, all she had was a cork-covered den door to keep out the noise while I studied. The fact that she put up with this for several years was a real act of love and sacrifice. No married person should enter graduate school unless they have such a tolerant and loving mate! Robert Orpen so aptly described our situation, "There are days when it takes all you've got just to keep up with the losers."

Fortunately, the military was interested in investigating the relationship between job satisfaction and performance and encouraged cross-country participation in a study. This became the primary thesis focus. Access to the units clerical and computer resources greatly assisted data analysis. Finally, I reached the apex of my academic aspirations. My wife, and my children, who so unstintingly supported me, were at my side to witness the granting of the degree. My only regret was that my parents, who did so much for me and had asked so little, were long deceased and could not be there to enjoy the fruits of their love and commitment. I vividly remember being asked, by a BA degree candidate, what it felt like to reach the top. Without hesitation I replied, "I am finally liberated from a life time ambition." An odd comment perhaps, but that was how I felt! Strangely also, I remember thinking how little I really knew. It was almost as if I was flying under false colours and someone would find out.

Two cows were grazing alongside a highway when a tank truck of milk on its way to the distributor happened to pass by. On one side of the truck in big red letters was a sign which read, "pasteurized, homogenized, standardized, vitamin A added." One cow turned to the other and remarked, "makes you feel sort of inadequate, doesn't it?"

Jacob M. Braude

Chapter Fourteen
A Time of Decision

For a period, life returned to normal. I was glad to have time to redeem myself with my family and do routine work, free of undue stress. Several events, however, led me to re-examine my suitability for an ongoing military career.

My work on motivation, job satisfaction and performance had become well known. This led to my being invited to give a paper on the subject to officers undergoing training for senior positions at the Canadian Forces Staff College. My senior, as head of the unit, let it be known that he should give the presentation. The Staff College, not wishing to give offence but wanting me to speak, elected to withdraw the invitation. Not only was I denied the opportunity for personal satisfaction and acclaim, but the unit as a whole forfeited the chance to publicize its expertise. Once again I was denied what was rightfully mine. My resentment returned to the forefront!

Shortly thereafter, I was asked to report to Military Headquarters to brief the General on my findings. On my arrival at headquarters I was told that the director would do the briefing with me in attendance as an underling. Again, I felt I was back to where my credibility needed enhancing by a higher rank. My superior attempted to do the presentation. In the process, due to a lack of expertise, he misconstrued the data, which led to confusion. The General, knowing I was the author of the study, in frustration turned to me, and asked that I clarify what was being said — and I did. Nevertheless, the episode left me embarrassed and resentful.

> For every door that closes there is
> another that will slam in your face.
> *Syd Handysides*

The same officer, being about a foot taller and overweight, often took great pleasure in ridiculing my size in front of others. This day, in the presence of a large audience of my peers, he repeated the performance. Still smarting from my previous embarrassment and recollecting similar distasteful episodes, I lost my cool. I exploded, saying, "when men are being measured this is done from the eyebrows up." A red-faced response, accompanied by loud guffaws, did not improve future relationships but at least broke the behaviour pattern. From my observation, many middle level, older officers relied unduly on their rank to carry the day especially when dealing with those younger than them. Perhaps their very attitude was the undoing of them. Nevertheless they often served as barriers to progress.

> No person can be a great leader unless he takes
> genuine joy in the success of those under him.
> *W. A. Nance*

I returned to my unit with reduced enthusiasm. The final blow soon followed. Some time later, rather than phone me, the Colonel sent a Corporal down the hall and summoned me to his office. On arrival, the Colonel informed me that the other co-ordinator, who was present and was junior to me, was being promoted to Lt Colonel ahead of me. I was assured that I was next to be promoted. Not being told this in private was both annoying and humiliating. I subsequently discovered that qualification as a pilot, which I lacked, made the difference. Rightly or wrongly, since the Colonel was also a pilot, I questioned his objectivity.

The time for in-depth evaluation had come. I felt I was locked in a history-driven system, which would always curtail achievement and satisfaction. More importantly, I concluded that I was not appreciated for what I could do, nor would I be allowed to utilize my skills to the fullest. In evaluating many of those in a leadership position, I was reminded of the appropriateness of the assessment of a senior officer recorded at the turn of the century, "Troops will follow this officer into battle out of sheer curiosity." This was not a situation with a promising future.

I also disagreed with the thrust of the unit, which focused heavily on doing applied research with little emphasis on marketing the results. Operational units were faced with a host of human problems requiring resolution and the unit, I believed, was ideally suited to providing such a consulting service. The commanding officer was not of that opinion. I believed a golden opportunity was being lost in which I would have enjoyed participating. Interestingly, when the budget crunch came, the unit's usefulness was questioned and in due course ceased to exist.

There was little doubt that a promotion was due shortly but my enthusiasm and commitment was waning. I began to think that the military was no longer for me. My family was quite young and were I to stay until retirement age, I would be returning to civilian life at a less marketable age. Just hanging around until pension time had little appeal. Life had much more to offer.

Many people's tombstones should read, Died at 30. Buried at 60.
Nicholas Murray Butler

Many factors required consideration were I to leave the military. I had security and the assurance of a forthcoming promotion. Were I to remain two additional years I would receive a pension for life. Since the military had also subsidized me to attend university, I would be obliged to reimburse the Crown for a portion of the funds expended on my education — a very fair expectation. The monies I had contributed to the pension plan would be returned without interest — all pension benefits would be forfeited. Moving from a base of security to uncertainty was a primary deterrent. What if I failed? There was no going back. By then I had four young children and their future would be impaired were I unsuccessful. I, however, encountered too many officers who hated what they were doing, longed to escape, but were too fearful to leave. I did not wish to have that happen to me. I could easily become embittered if I stayed. Consequently, I began looking elsewhere for employment.

While dissatisfied with the circumstances facing me, I owed the military a great deal. There are few organizations who so effectively teach leadership, responsibility, administration and self-confidence — very transferable skills. As a military officer, I had the opportunity to choose work I truly enjoyed, and which became my career focus. The generous financial support and time off to attend university provided the skills and credentials needed to enter other fields of endeavour. For this I am grateful. I was always proud to be a military officer, an experience that greatly enriched my life. I still get choked up when observing Memorial Day services.

If you think old soldiers just fade away,
try getting into your old army uniform.
Jacob M Braude Treasury

Chapter Fifteen
Leaving the Military

The decision having been made to leave the military, I began searching for challenging employment. Two universities offered teaching appointments but they were not to my liking. Exploring other opportunities, I became aware that a Community College was being started in Edmonton. Educational thrusts by such institutions approximated the kind of teaching I had done in the military and seemed less ethereal than a university.

The designated new College president was still filling a comparable position in Toronto. I made an appointment to see him, and forwarded my credentials to him in advance. A burly aggressive man, who towered over me, seemed unimpressed with my dossier. During the course of the interview he aggressively stated, "I can get people with your credentials a dime a dozen." I felt as if I was back in the military and reacted in my accustomed way saying, "Like hell you can! I've got a perfectly good job with a promising future and I am only looking to see if you can offer me something better." Big John laughed and the interview was terminated. I was convinced that I would hear no more from him. At least I had the satisfaction of not having been intimidated by his aggressiveness. There is a time to stand up and be yourself. No one can do it for you.

A Journey Through Inadequacy

A few days later, John called and offered me the position of assistant chairman. While the title was promising, the starting salary was less than that of a Major. Furthermore, I would be on probation until I could prove my wares. I also had to pay the relocation costs as well as reimburse the military for my education. The uncertainty, stress and strain that would be imposed on my wife and family was a major deterrent. Few husbands were blessed with such a loving and supportive wife as mine. She was prepared to go along with my decision even though she would have preferred that I stay in the military, or accept a professorship in Toronto.

The greatest happiness of life is the conviction that we are loved
— loved for ourselves, or rather loved in spite of ourselves.
Victor Hugo

There were however, positive attractions. I believed my training as a military officer and my experience as an administrator would quickly lead to advancement. Presumptuous and risky perhaps — but I believed it. The absence of well ingrained programs and systems offered a great deal of flexibility, not available to me in the military. There was the added attraction that Edmonton was where I wanted to be if I wished to become active in politics managing my brother-in-law's campaign for election as a Member of Parliament. A major determiner was the president who had interviewed me. I concluded that anyone who allowed me to be as outspoken as I had been, was someone I would enjoy working with. This proved to be the case. Overall there was the attraction of a challenging new career in a promising setting.

After a short deliberation, I phoned John and accepted the appointment. This triggered a range of events commencing with the sale of our house. I was needed on site since the College was to open in a few months. Programs required development, budgets prepared for government approval, and staff hired to deliver offerings. This left my wife with the task of selling our home — a tedious task to say the least. Previous sales had well acquainted us with real estate agent expectations as well as client insensitivities. There was the ongoing need to keep the house tidy, stay clear when clients were brought in, smile when children tracked mud throughout the house, remain calm when people complained about the lack of a fire place or the shortage of bathrooms, which they insisted on flushing repeatedly, and responding to insulting purchase offers when we sincerely believed we owned the Taj Mahal.

God gives burdens; also shoulders.

Jimmy Carter

Chapter Sixteen
Life in the Academic World

Ileft the military and arrived in Edmonton to take up my position, on the sixth of June, which I felt was appropriate — the historic World War 2 — D-Day. My arrival was in the midst of chaotic activity. We were in temporary quarters with no office for me, only a desk and a chair, which someone seized when I went to the washroom. Not only that, the faculty gradually being hired, knew everything about everything, and had little respect for authority. I had just come from a background where my juniors stood to attention as they entered my office. The sudden change was startling to say the least. I could no longer depend on rank, but was obliged to rely entirely on persuasive and performance skills. I was reminded of the old adage: When people's needs are met they get on the bandwagon.

There were many moments when I questioned the rashness of my decision and longed for the security of the military. But there was no turning back! To complicate matters, my immediate senior seemed equally overwhelmed and provided little assistance. I was left entirely on my own. The old sink or swim survival approach came into play. In the military I had never been responsible for funds nor had budget preparation been one of my duties. Suddenly, I was expected to prepare budgets in support of programs which ran into the millions. I suppose, at this point, some of my previous banking experience proved helpful. Additionally, my graduate school training in research and experience as a military officer conducting military evaluation studies were of great assistance. Once I overcame my initial fright, I discovered that budgeting was systematic and logical. Furthermore, no one knew any more about the process than I did — a real source of comfort! When other College departments adopted my approach to budgeting, I was no longer intimidated.

Moving into an entirely new arena is both threatening and stimulating. It certainly tests one's survival skills as well as provides new opportunities for growth and development, so crucial to revitalization. My background in research, both at graduate school and in the military, provided the foundation for new program development and implementation. My training in administration and experience in public speaking equipped me with the skills and confidence needed to sell what I had developed. For this I owe the military a debt of gratitude. The opening of the College, which had been a food store, was several weeks behind schedule. My office was immediately above what was formerly the meat department. This must have some underlying significance! The hectic pace quickly erased any recollection of the military with which I had been so engrossed over many years.

When we accept tough jobs as a challenge to our ability
and wade into them with joy, miracles can happen.
Arland Gilbert

One of the initial attractions to the academic world was the opportunity to teach and update myself in my discipline. This lasted one term! Six months after the launching of the institution, my superior elected to leave and the position of Campus Director became available. I decided to enter the fray and was selected. Responsibility for campus facilities as well as programming was an entirely new challenge; especially since I had just gotten my feet wet. Errors in judgement were quickly brought to my attention especially by faculty in areas where I had no expertise.

One humorous episode comes to mind. A very large program head stomped into my office and, towering over me with upraised fist, expressed his displeasure. What the important issue was, I cannot remember. On my retirement, my former secretary reminded me of my long forgotten response. Apparently, I got up on my chair and told Bob to come closer so I could kick him in the ass. This non-conventional response appealed to his sense of humour. He left, and laughingly waved his fist as he walked down the hall. From that point onward we got along well.

> Men show their character in nothing more clearly than by
> what they think laughable.
>
> *Goethe*

When one feels insecure advice is frequently sought — a healthy, normal reaction. Too often we overlook what is available at our doorstep. Unfortunately, we too frequently associate good advice with the position of the advisor, hoping the advice giver's status will carry the day.

As a Campus Director I received some of the best advice from an unusual source, the head custodian. Olga was a bright, insightful lady who had her finger on the pulse of the campus. She also had very well developed interpersonal skills. Everyone liked her and freely shared their views and concerns with her as she moved from office to office. She could have been my mother and she treated me like a son. Once a week I went down to her little office next to the cleaning equipment where we shared coffee and her home-made cookies. Over time we developed a close trusting relationship. Olga kept me abreast of potential problem areas and sore points that she had noticed, which I took to heart. Quite often she expressed the opinion that I was out in left field on some issues. Knowing all this provided me with insights unavailable through other sources and helped me nip many potential problems in the bud. To this day we are still friends.

> *There is nothing we receive with so much reluctance as advice.*
> *Joseph Addison*

There was something exciting about being part of a new evolving organization. During the formative years one knew everyone and supportive relationships were easily developed since we depended on each other. Gradually, as the institution grew, this was lost and a note of formality crept in, especially as new campuses were developed. Attention became focused on divisions and departments with the individual assuming less significance. It was at this point that I found leadership assumed special significance.

An exciting moment came when I was appointed Dean. Some of the spark of newness returned. My appointment provided the opportunity to explore and develop new areas. Taking Diploma programs off campus to Aboriginal communities was especially rewarding since they were much needed and were greatly appreciated. Often, in providing such services, I was reminded of my one-room rural school beginnings. Perhaps my background helped me to relate. My various experiences with feelings of inadequacy provided insights that words could not describe and gained acceptance — a most rewarding and humbling experience. Another special interest of mine was the provision of life-enriching learning experiences for older adults which I hoped to develop later.

Chapter Seventeen
Diversions

Politics

One of my additional reasons for coming to Edmonton was to become involved in politics. Shortly after my arrival, my brother-in-law decided to run on a Liberal ticket and asked me to be his campaign manager, at a time when Prime Minister Trudeau's image was at an all time low. Once again my lack of familiarity with the ins and outs of politics readily became apparent. I somehow expected it to be a lofty experience focusing on service to the country with the best man emerging as the victor. Quickly I discovered that it was a blood sport with character assassination the order of the day. Political forums designed to familiarize the public with candidate's character, skills and policies, often were fraudulent exercises. Forums were packed with loyal candidate supporters who asked questions that made their candidate look good and the opposition inferior. One election was won by a local pig farmer who had no knowledge of the country beyond the Alberta borders let alone other parts of the world. The local newspaper reporting results commented that a piece of wood, providing it was with the right party, could have won. My reputation as a campaign manager was not enhanced by the outcome. Three subsequent failures confirmed my incompetence as a political strategist. At least I had the good sense to stay clear of politics after that. Several experiences stayed with me. I met Mr. Trudeau on two separate occasions and was impressed with his capacity to make one feel you were the only person of importance during the brief time he talked to you. Not so most others — I specifically recall being introduced to a cabinet minister who kept looking over my head at the crowd to see if there was any one of greater importance nearby — not an elevating experience. On another occasion the president of the College, who had once been involved in managing Lester Pearson's prime ministerial campaign, phoned the campus where a meeting of senior officers was taking place. My secretary answered the phone and was completely taken in by John who put on a French accent, saying he was Prime Minister Trudeau and wished to talk to me. Laurene came downstairs and passed on the message. I was sitting beside a status-conscious lady to whom I commented, "If the Prime Minister wants me I guess I better go." On picking up the phone I was greeted by gales of laughter by the President who had his chuckle for the day. Taking advantage of the image that I was in contact with the Prime Minister, I never corrected the misperception with the status-conscious lady. Some rumours are best nurtured! Despite these experiences I still hold the democratic process in high regard and would highly encourage committed people to throw their hat in the ring. More people of substance are needed.

Find a purpose in life so big it will challenge
every capacity to be at your best.
David O. McKay

Venture Into Business

I had always been attracted by the possibility of establishing my own personnel consulting company. When an opportunity came along to undertake a major study on retirement in Alberta, sponsored by the Provincial government, I took the job. This developed into a consulting business. Two services were developed: research and personnel selection and placement. I lacked the courage to go into this area full time which would have meant leaving the secure position of College Dean. Rather, I erroneously assumed I could do this as a sideline relying on others to do the day to day work under my distant supervision. I soon discovered that potential clients were reluctant to do business without the assurance of the full time involvement of the principle player. Furthermore, an integrated team approach was needed where diversity of involvement was a financial necessity. Unfortunately, those doing research took a purist, academic approach avoiding all participation in perceived mundane activities, which paid the rent. This they viewed as demeaning, not in keeping with their professional training. My not being there on a regular basis prevented the establishment of the necessary linkage.

To complicate matters, I naively decided to expand my business activities. The shopping centre in which my consulting services was located had a space which they wished developed as a coffee, tea and spice shop. Once again, despite my wife's sage advice, I jumped at the opportunity and became a shopkeeper. Again, I relied on the services of others to do the day to day work — a ridiculous assumption. Those involved lacked the claimed expertise, displayed little commitment, and theft became a problem. The only solution was more family control. Consequently, my wife was suddenly obliged to cut back on her nursing career and take over day to day operations — which she did exceedingly well in spite of a lack of interest. When an opportunity to open a second shop in another mall presented itself, I grabbed it, not having learned from experience. The rationale for doing this was the belief that our four children could help out and would profit from the experience. This was partly true, but in due course they wished to pursue other interests away from parental control. Nevertheless, they all learned what it was like to be in business and the work required to do well. There was the additional benefit of being exposed to demanding, inconsiderate people and learning how to deal with them. This was quite different from talking back to a tolerant parent.

Get your priorities right — No one ever said on his death bed, "Gee if I'd only spent more time at the office."
Readers Digest — *Author unknown*

Looking back, I am led to wonder how I could have become so involved in so many things without realizing there would be negative consequences. Fortunately, even though quality family time was sacrificed, we survived but this was due primarily to the efforts of my long-suffering and loving wife. Even at this point in my life I still hadn't overcome my feelings of inadequacy; I still had to shore up that fragile self-image with unrealistic accomplishments. It was at this time that I gave the graduation address to a class of nurses. My topic was, "Take time out to smell the roses." On the way home from the function I asked Sel what she thought of my speech. She replied, "It was very good, you should read it some time." This comment rocked me to my socks and began a self-evaluation process, which took some time to reach fruition. At the same time, a faculty member, with whom I had previously clashed over an academic matter, told a local paper that I was spending more time at my other interests than on the job as Dean. A simultaneous incentive was the growing indebtedness of the consulting business which could lead to bankruptcy. When an offer to buy emerged, I gratefully sold. It was at this time that my wife gave me a framed memento, written by Henri Frederic Amiel, which touched me deeply. It said, "It is not what he has which directly expresses the worth of a man, but what he is."

Shortly thereafter, we sold one shop and concentrated on the other, which still remained my wife's responsibility. When it was eventually sold, just prior to one Christmas, Sel commented that it was like being released from prison. If there was ever a saint tolerating my escapades — she was it! It is so easy to get caught up in ambition without Realizing the motivating source.

Later on, unencumbered by the need to achieve, I realized that I still hadn't shed the perceptions of my past; the unconscious feelings that I still wasn't quite worthwhile; that I had to shore up my self image. Somehow, when one is in the midst of the fray it is hard to be analytical; in fact one avoids doing so since it would compel one to take a different course of action. Jules Z. Willing captures this, "Man can persuade himself that his sacrifices were made in order to provide for his wife and children."

Chapter Eighteen
Returning to Academia

Eccentric Professors: Academia Nuts

Mike Millard

I used to think that all the odd balls were in the military and was somewhat surprised to see the same behaviour reflected in academics. Somehow, naively, I expected them to be more scholarly, more altruistic, rising above the frailness of human behaviour. That this was not so became very apparent when there was a change of presidents and the new arrival, wishing to gain acceptance, became a vulnerable victim of faculty misrepresentations. Two vociferous chairmen strongly disagreed with the priorities I had established for the division, especially with regard to the distribution of funds. Other departments, they believed, were less worthy of the support I was giving them. Whatever their motives, they chose to demean me in the eyes of the new President to the point where he expressed doubts about my abilities as an administrator.

This lack of support almost pulled the props from under me. My confidence was shaken! I had left a promising military career believing I could make my mark in the academic community. This perception had been shared by the former president and was reinforced by informal feedback from others. The time had come for me to "fish or cut bait." Needless to say, the threat was almost over-powering. At this point, training to cope with adversity acquired as a military officer came into play. I aggressively told the president that I believed I was his best administrator and demanded the right to prove this. At my insistence, we agreed to an across-college evaluation of my performance and perceived abilities with input from all levels: faculty, support staff and senior administrators. This was to be conducted by the external Research Department. To say I wasn't anxious would be a gross understatement. Failure would tarnish my reputation not only within the College but also with my family and the outside community. I prayerfully hoped for the best. At that point I was grateful that I had a sideline business I could fall back on in the event the tide turned against me.

When life is kicking you in the teeth, become a dentist.
Keven Meyers

The day to cut the mustard came. The Vice President sat down with me to review the results, which were noteworthy in their consistency. With the exception of two input sources, whom we both knew were the instigators, I earned outstanding evaluations. I was overcome with relief and thanks. The Good Lord hears prayers! I insisted that the evaluation results be reviewed with the President who had to accept the findings without expressing regrets for having doubted my ability. To his credit, however, my annual evaluations thereafter were exemplary and these were approved by him. I'm certain that all my past strivings and the experience gained from struggling with adversity prepared me well for this momentous occasion. Without this seasoning I would never have survived to see a better day!

What amazed me was the resilience of those who attempted to do me in. At our regular face to face meetings they displayed no signs of discomfort or regret. One of the perpetrators frequently told me, with seeming sincerity, that he was one of my staunchest and most loyal supporters.

Once again my naivety had dominated. You would think with all my training in human behaviour and my experience with people, I would have had greater insight. Reflecting on this, and in defense of myself, I have concluded that most people are honourable and to think otherwise would turn one into a cynic. Better to be stung now and again than to become a negative person and assume no one can be taken at face value.

Dogs are much like people. Usually only one in a group is barking at something in particular; the others are barking at him.

John M. Henry

Overall the faculty were creative and committed teachers who cared for their students. Nevertheless, as in any organization, there were misfits who provide the spice of life.

The initial President had a special interest in horses, which led to the launching of an Equine program. Administrative problems led to staff changes resulting in the reassignment of the program to me as one of my responsibilities. It is somewhat ironical that I, who had struggled so hard to get off the farm, once again found myself blessed with animal husbandry responsibilities. The first requirement was to hire someone familiar with Equine Studies who could also administer the program. My expertise was limited to the farm, riding horses bareback. With this in mind, I assembled a selection committee to choose the best from a list of applicants. Since the President saw himself as an authority in the equine field, I imposed on him to lend his expertise. As a psychologist, I felt well qualified to evaluate the human dimension. A nursing head and another senior administrator formed the decision-making group.

Looking back on the reliance on my own expertise I was reminded of a story, whose author I could not remember, that so well described the danger of doing so. This fellow had spent his entire life studying goldfish. At a meeting of Goldfish Lovers of America he was asked how one could tell the difference between male and female goldfish. "That's simple," said the man of knowledge, "male goldfish will eat male worms." But persisted the questioner, "Can you tell the difference between male and female worms?" "Haven't the slightest idea," he replied. "I'm not an expert on worms — just goldfish."

Several candidates were interviewed with attention focused on a middle-aged flashy lady with claimed extensive horsemanship experience and academic credentials at the Ph.D. level. All but the nursing instructor were impressed. While she couldn't provide specific reasons for her distrust, she remained adamant in her opinion. Nevertheless, the view of the majority ruled and the decision was made to extend an offer of employment. This task was left to me. I phoned the successful candidate at her new location in another city and was taken back by her lack of enthusiasm. She said that she had just relocated, had hung up her pictures in a recently acquired residence and wasn't too enthusiastic about repeating the process. I, on the other hand, fearing a live one was about to slip away and that I would be stuck with running the program, applied all my persuasive skills. Finally, after considerable arm twisting, she reluctantly agreed to give it a try for a year. I was elated that a major problem had been solved. Little did I realize what the future would bring.

The day of her arrival was anticipated with considerable enthusiasm on my part. When she phoned to announce her presence, as a good administrator, I put out the welcome mat and invited her for drinks and dinner. An impressive, bumptious, highly confident bleached blond bounced in. When I introduced her to my wife as the learned doctor and equine expert, she cavalierly asked that she be addressed by her first name. My wife, a very experienced nurse who appreciates the bizarre later commented, "Just imagine me — a simple little housewife being on first name basis with a doctor."

At the time I was also responsible for Performing and Design Arts. I referred to them as the prancers and dancers and I included the Equine

Program under the same umbrella. This being so, non-conventional behaviour was considered the norm. When the new equine head displayed quaint behaviour, I was not surprised since this fit in with my expectations. Furthermore, I assumed it would take her a semester or two to adjust.

When assigned an office, to the annoyance of her peers, she insisted that her nameplate be replaced with one that included the title — Dr. During our regular meetings, conversation on academic matters simply lacked substance. For example, when I questioned if the program could be reduced by one semester, she came back in a few hours with program revisions which, even to an equine novitiate, didn't make sense. In due course, feedback from staff and the equine community generated grounds for concern. People commented that her knowledge base was superficial and her riding skills were at the layman level.

During a dinner event at our home, claims to fame related to my wife and daughter lacked credibility. She, for example, claimed that her mother had taught thirteen languages at university. My wife later commented that perhaps twelve but not thirteen. In a conversation with my daughter, who was sixteen at the time, she claimed to have ridden against Princess Anne but had lost. She further stated that she had competed at Wimbledon but when questioned as to who she had played against, could not remember. My daughter, who followed tennis closely, later commented that this could not be true; you simply do not forget such a momentous event. She, in fact, was the first to cast doubt on our esteemed guest. To top it all off, her supposed undercover work with the American Secret Service caused my wife to wince. I dismissed the concern saying people do interesting things! Actually, I simply didn't wish to face the fact that I had a problem that had to be solved.

Other incidents finally brought things to a head. Although the lady claimed an MBA, a review of her budget presentation reflected a total lack of understanding of what was required. Even simple figures didn't add up. A visit by the owner of the riding stable we rented for program use, added to my problems. He described behaviour of a personal nature involving students that demanded action. I vividly remember phoning the President and advising him of the various happenings, leading me to conclude that we had a deranged person or a fraud on our hands and that I would be taking appropriate action. He was only too glad to leave matters in my hands. The fact that he had been part of the selection committee was not discussed.

The Human Resources Department, being very new, had not established a policy requiring all faculty to validate their claimed credentials. I decided to start there. I phoned the University of British Columbia who had no record of the lady ever having earned a BA. I next checked out the claimed MBA from Washington University, with similar results. My discussions with the registrar at South Hampton University, UK, produced an interesting response. The registrar stated that they did not have a graduation on that date. The British always did have a unique knack of saying negative things in the most diplomatic way.

The dye having been cast, action was required. I briefed the Director of Human Resources on the situation and asked him to sit in on the confrontation interview to validate discussions. The self-described learned lady was brought in and simply told that the credentials she claimed were not substantiated by the universities I had contacted. She displayed tremendous aplomb. Self assuredly she acknowledged that the credentials were not in her name. This was because her husband had done some dastardly deeds and she wished to disassociate herself from him and these events. Consequently, the credentials claimed were in another name. She said it so convincingly that, until I had a grip on myself, I was almost inclined to believe her. Fortunately, rational thinking prevailed. I decided to call her bluff stating that unless she promptly provided proof to the contrary, she had until noon to get off the campus. The Director of Human Resources was asked to accompany her to her office to obtain documentation or help her clean out her office. High noon came and to my relief she departed. Later I discovered she had left town with an assortment of equine equipment. I was all for sending the cops on her tail but the President felt the adverse publicity would only harm the College.

I wasn't quite finished with the lady. I received numerous calls from people such as bank managers, rental agents, etc, who had been fleeced by her cunning. I could take some comfort in knowing I wasn't the only one who had been sucked in! A final brash act. The faculty just prior to this had negotiated a contract which granted extra pay for advanced degrees. Lo and behold, one evening I received a long distance call from my defrocked friend demanding back pay in accordance with her phoney credentials. I hung up and that was the last I ever heard of her.

I had always been fascinated by the antics of Ferdinand Demara, the Great Impostor, who similarly, without any credentials became a university professor, and an assistant warden at a prison, just to mention a few accomplishments. On more than one occasion, I had commented that it would have been fascinating to have known such a person yet I failed to recognize his kinfolk when I had her on staff — so much for psychological training! The episode became the talk of the College and on many retreats I was obliged to repeat the story to the amusement of all. The Christmas after she left I received the doctor's nameplate, nicely wrapped, a gift from the Director of Plant and Development. I still have it in my garage as a reminder of past failures.

Somehow this program remained a problem until the end. One faculty member had long fingers that routinely extended into the petty cash box. Not being sufficiently rewarding, the theft of hay on the way to the centre was an additional accomplishment. Eventually, I convinced the Board to transfer the program to an agricultural college where it should have been in the first instance. Even then I was accused of unloading second class nags which they had received at no cost. I still get contractions in my stomach when I drive by equine establishments.

Everything is funny as long as
it happens to someone else.

Will Rogers

There are other happenings of interest but there is one that stands out in my mind since I managed to nip it in the bud. A faculty member desiring a doctorate in Psychology decided to enrol in a self-study distance delivery program offered by an institution of questionable reputation similar to those that offer wrestling diplomas by correspondence. As Psychology was my area of training, I was especially interested in the curriculum. A requirement for the degree was the completion of an abbreviated thesis. Through the grapevine I heard that he was doing something in the area of older adult education. I had recently completed a thorough review of the literature in the field supplemented by visits to various countries and incorporated in a report. A study comparison, consequently, was of special interest to me. With this in mind, I asked to read a draft copy of the thesis. On reading what was reluctantly submitted, I was astonished to discover that with only minor modifications; it was a copy of my study. When I pointed this out, the faculty member brazenly commented, "Isn't it amazing how similar they are." With considerable vigour, I stated that were he to submit this as his thesis I would consider this plagiarism and disciplinary action would be taken.

I never did learn how the thesis requirements were met. In due course, however, he waved a document in my face declaring him the holder of a Ph.D. With this in hand he demanded that appropriate salary adjustments be made. I was not prepared to do this but, since I would be seen as biased, I referred the credential to the local university for evaluation. The registrar's office concluded that they wouldn't even equate at the Master's level. This information did not sit well with the faculty member.

Every profession has its share of oddballs and perhaps misfits. That's what provides local colour and taste. I am reminded of a Philosophy instructor who fit the bill. He was interviewed on TV as a representative sample of people involved in post secondary education.

When asked what he did, he condescendingly replied that he was a "professional thinker." The body language of the interviewer said it all. I'm sure she reflected the views of the public; resentment at the patronizing implication that only philosophers have the capacity to think. One is reminded of the old proverb, "Pride cometh before the fall." Interestingly, students viewed him with great favour. His anti-establishment ways appealed to the naive youth who worshipped at the altar of academia; the font of all knowledge! Montaign well described the fallacy of such egotism, "You can be erudite with the knowledge of others; you can be wise only with your own wisdom."

The vast majority of faculty were well qualified, excellent teachers who were very committed to their students. This was evident in the number of outreach offerings made available to disadvantaged populations. The Social Work program, for example, graduated more aboriginal students with diplomas in Social Work than any other educational institution in the province — a real tribute to the faculty. I felt honoured to be the Dean. Stating faculty were strong willed, committed to their beliefs is an under-statement. This was especially evident at budget time when the gloves were taken off. It was a practical expectation that chairpersons would present the strongest case for their departments. Such support, nevertheless, was there when I, likewise, fought for a piece of the College pie. My role was to ensure the fair distribution of resources. This often put me in a conflict situation. But, when given a choice of implementing alternate processes, none were forthcoming.

I came to realize that budget time allowed for therapeutic ventilation with me being the target. Nevertheless, I felt highly honoured when they expressed the belief that no other administrator could get a bigger piece of the pie.

Some people think that living within a budget
is a fate worse than debt.
Toronto Globe and Mail

Even though distanced from the faculty, I felt I was accepted. I was especially touched when on various social occasions they felt free to perform skits exploiting my eccentricities; which were numerous. One year the faculty nominated me for the College medallion for outstanding service. Some eight years after retirement a large number of staff invited me to a recognition luncheon claiming they previously lacked the opportunity to say good bye and express their thanks for what I had done for them as Dean. These were very touching occasions that finally led me to believe I had balanced my inadequacies with accomplishments. I also had grown to accept the fact that mankind will always be marked with imperfection and accepting this is very liberating.

Every achiever I have met says, "my life turned
around when I began to believe in me."
Robert Schuller

The College had gone through interesting stages in its development. When I first arrived as an assistant chairman, it had just been launched. There were no buildings and no programs. Only the Board of Governors and the President had been appointed with the stipulation that the institution was to be up and running in six months. I was in the right place at the right time. I had left the military because I no longer believed I was in a position to make a difference; that I no longer had the chance to contribute in a worthwhile way applying what I had learned at graduate school. This certainly was not the case at the College. I quickly became a vital link in launching the College. It was an exciting time providing the challenge I needed. I certainly didn't have time to become encumbered by a mid-life crisis. I almost felt that I had been robbed of the experience.

The first years were exciting times. Since the institution was small, one knew everyone on a first name basis. Processes, rules and procedures were still being developed and most decisions were verbally agreed to with paper work minimized. Rapid growth necessitated the introduction of rules and regulations, which gradually restricted independence of operation. Nevertheless, as Dean, I enjoyed the luxury of relative independence. This provided the opportunity to launch programs in traditionally neglected areas.

Servicing the Aboriginal community became a primary thrust of our division. I quickly learned that one had to gain acceptance with this group. The status associated with an academic institution meant little. One was obliged to earn one's spurs but this proved to be a rewarding challenge. Academic credentials, many an instructor discovered, meant little unless one was accepted. Accidental happenings often tipped the scales. At one campus meeting with Aboriginal elders, I discovered that one of the elders, Alice, had her cheque rejected at a local bank because, supposedly, she was unknown. I took her back to the bank, vouched for her, and the cheque was cashed. From that time onward she accepted me. The importance of this was so evident when I was planning a large conference on Aboriginal education. A meeting had been set up with all the Aboriginal leaders. I arrived early but was ignored until Alice arrived. She invited me to the table and from that moment onward I became part of the group. Incidentally, the conference, run primarily by the Aboriginal community, was a great success.

I was especially interested in providing life enriching learning experiences for older adults. My parents typified a generation whom, due to financial and family obligations, were denied the educational opportunities available to their children. They were as bright as their children and much interested in learning. Unfortunately, that generation came to believe that education was for their children and time had passed them by. Indeed, in many instances they were intimidated by educational institutions. Ours, also, is a youth-oriented society that sees little value in educating those who are out of the work force. There exists the belief that spending educational funds on seniors cannot be justified even though endless studies reinforce the belief that a stimulated person is a much healthier cost-effective person. Easily forgotten is the fact that these older adults built this nation. It was their sacrifices that made the country what it is. This being so, should they be denied stimulating learning experiences? I felt strongly that this was their entitlement.

With this in mind, I dreamt of establishing a Senior Studies Institute under the College umbrella. I convinced my administrative peers to allot some surplus funds to researching this possibility. With the help of an assistant, we researched the literature ascertaining what had been done in other North American institutions. This was supplemented by visits to leading educational establishments in the United States, Germany, Sweden and the United Kingdom. The best of all the centres visited was located in Bedford, England. Success was attributable to the imagination, leadership and commitment of the director.

Touring the centre one day I encountered a man coming out of a room with tears streaming from his eyes. I remember wondering what they were doing to that poor man only to discover that he was taking a cooking class for men and had been exposed to a large dose of onion fumes. The incident, however, stayed with me and led me to wonder why we didn't offer similar training for widowers, suddenly left to fend for themselves, rather than make them unduly dependent on others. An old friend once said that anyone who can read can cook — so also widowers. Such training needs could readily be met by technical institutions who would enhance their image by doing so. A Senior Studies Institute could do likewise.

Findings were incorporated in a report, reviewed and endorsed by senior administration. A subsequent recommendation to establish a Senior Studies Institute was submitted to the Board of Governors. I came to the Board well prepared to defend the recommendation. Before I was given the opportunity to make my case, a Board member asked to speak. I fully expected the traditional strong renunciation. To my amazement the member commented that this was the best idea ever to hit the College and he moved acceptance. To my delight approval was granted. I was almost disappointed that I was denied the chance to make my pitch. Fortunately, I had the sense to keep quiet. There was the proviso that the Institute would be self-supporting, and I would be held accountable for fund raising. Once again I was reminded of the importance of having a dream and pursuing it.

Launching the Institute was one of my most rewarding life experiences. Although it involved endless hours soliciting funds, I felt privileged to give something back to those who had gone before. Those approached for funding could readily relate since they had elderly parents or eventually would be going that way. As funds were acquired, interest grew. By the time I left the College some $650,000 had been acquired and put into an interest bearing account.

What was most rewarding was older adult participation. Many gave freely of their time performing numerous teaching and support functions. Others registered in courses with no entrance requirements other than the desire for learning. Several thousand older adults registered in the courses. Well-attended educational travel trips were arranged tying into educational institutions in France, Greece, the United Kingdom and China. Many who participated had never travelled before but were comfortable doing so under a College protective umbrella provided by Liela, the Institute co-ordinator. Both employees and volunteers shared their delight and the opportunity to enhance their self-image doing something for others. One is reminded of the comment that, "One should live life in such a way that the preacher can tell the truth at your funeral."

Financial constraints gradually led to fee increases and programming cutbacks. Many lower income seniors could no longer afford the increased registration fees. For the Institute to remain self-supporting, as originally intended, ongoing fund raising was needed. Unfortunately, other priorities assumed greater importance.

With Provincial cutbacks, educational funding was markedly reduced. Where formerly the focus was on growth and development, the emphasis shifted to cut backs and conservation. Survival and maintenance became the primary concern. What was once new and invigorating was becoming staid and traditional.

There was one bright spot that appeared on the horizon — the construction of a large downtown campus. Several years went into the planning. Construction was unique and complimented city hall and downtown facilities. My biggest argument was with the architect who strongly opposed my desire to incorporate a clock in the design. I eventually won and its addition adds to the image of an academic institution. Moving day came and faculty relocated to the new digs.

For me, the opportunity to take early retirement became available, and I decided to pursue a less stressful life and relocate to my home. Starting meetings at seven am, continuing long into the day with a full briefcase accompanying me home at night, had become burdensome. There were other things I wanted to do with my life and I realized I didn't have endless time. With my wife's input, we concluded that retirement could be rewarding. A friend advised us that we should travel before we were on a fracture board. We planned to follow through on this advice. Cary Grant's comment also rang home, "When people tell you how young you look, they are also telling you how old you are."

I left the College on a high note feeling my accomplishments were a culmination of satisfying life achievements. Few are so fortunate. It was time to pursue another career.

Chapter Nineteen
The Career of Retirement

Often I'm asked how I like retirement with the expectation that a dissatisfied response will be forthcoming. Many people express surprise when I respond saying, "It's the best job I have ever had."

When I first retired, I often felt the need to justify what I did with my time — almost as if I was obliged to give an accounting. Eventually, I learned not to offer a clarification but simply stated, "I do all the things you dream about." That rapidly brought questioning to a close. It took me a while to realize that others self-interest, their personal preoccupation with their own retirement, was behind the question — concern about my adjustment was of lesser importance.

I quickly learned that a retired person has diminished status. Society tends to reinforce this feeling of unworthiness by associating personal worth with the work one does. It is interesting to observe the interpersonal dynamics at social events. Invariably, once introductions have been completed and those in attendance break into smaller groups, one of the first questions asked is: what do you do for a living? Somehow people seem to need this information to commence meaningful conversation. They must know where to peg you to focus their chat. To exemplify — my daughter, married to a medical doctor who delivers many babies, was selling his truck. An interested buyer came to look at the vehicle when only my daughter was available. During preliminary discussions he asked, "What does your husband do?" To this my daughter responded, "He is in the delivery business." This made sense to the buyer who then continued with negotiations.

The work that you do relates to your personal worth. When you say you are retired, interest frequently dwindles and the questioner moves on to more fruitful fields. When this occurs, it is possible that one's self-image plummets accompanied by feelings of resentment, unworthiness and the temptation to reinstate yourself by describing what you did prior to retirement. But this lacks the status of a real job — it's ancient history.

You are more than your work and you are also
more than a set of golf clubs.

Stephen Pollan

I had done a great deal of research examining what people stated they were looking forward to on retirement and their actual experiences once they had retired. Consequently, I had a broad academic understanding of what was required for a fulfilling retirement. Despite all my previous learning and experience, it took a lengthy period for me to make a full adjustment. The old saying comes to mind: It is one thing to talk the talk but an entirely different thing to walk the talk. I had been so engrossed in my work that the abrupt change can be compared with withdrawal symptoms experienced by an addict. Where once I had a computer literate staff to assist me, I suddenly had no one. While I had planned to do some writing I couldn't type and computers were beyond me. Worse still, no one sought my advice. My world had done a complete turn around. I was reminded of a real life story I read about the Dean who had retired. His former secretary had also retired at the same time. A week after the Dean's departure he phoned back to his former office wishing to talk to his replacement. The new secretary asked for his name. Since it was a bit unusual, she asked him to spell it. So much for short lived status.

The first while I slept late and had lengthy naps in the afternoon to the point that my wife began to worry about my health — especially questioning whether I was depressed. Little did I realize that I was simply exhausted from the previous pace extending over many years. After several months, my energy returned leading me to start acquiring needed rehabilitation skills. I registered for a computer course but found the experience rather intimidating. Those in the class seemed to be tuned in and asked questions beyond my comprehension. I felt as if I was back as an undergraduate registered in the wrong program for which I simply lacked the aptitude. I opted for a safer route where my ineptitude would not become public — I purchased some computer books for dummies. Even then I felt the dummies had the edge on me. Gradually, through trial and error and much demoralizing persistence, I advanced from kindergarten to grade one. When I asked my children for assistance, they invariably dumped out buckets of computer knowledge beyond my comprehension. When they rolled their eyes upward with that, "I don't believe this" look, my anxiety and feelings of incompetence were magnified.

I went through a phase where I believed others, including family members, were relegating me to the scrap heap. I felt little significance was attributed to my views and that my expertise was no longer of consequence. This also was reflected in my interpersonal behaviour. One of my children expressed concern to her mother that I had become grumpy, somewhat intolerant, lacking the bounce previously evident, and had become somewhat insular. You would think that someone with my background, training and experience would have had the insight needed to modify such behaviour. This merely emphasizes human vulnerability regardless of background. I didn't stop to think that others were so preoccupied with the demands of their daily life

A Journey Through Inadequacy

that my adjustment challenges assumed far less importance. Furthermore, others had every reason to believe that I, being freed from the burdens of responsibility, should be on cloud nine.

> *The only things worth learning are the things*
> *you learn after you know it all.*
>
> *Harry S. Truman*

Prior to retirement I had given some thought to trying my hand at writing, but I began to question my ability to do so. I kept thinking it was rather presumptuous for me to believe that I had anything of consequence to say that would be of interest and helpful to others. It was better not to try than to do so and prove oneself unworthy. My most faithful devoted and loving friend, my wife Selma, kept reminding me that I could offer much and should get off my duff and do something about it. Many friends who I very much admired provided the nurturing feedback I needed.

As a first step, I initiated a research project in which I volunteered to do a study for our District Church Executive involving a job analysis of executive functions as well as investigating training needs for serving pastors. This extended over several years and proved to be quite successful, as well as satisfying my need for creativity and achievement. I discovered I hadn't lost my touch and could be productive in a new setting. A long-standing friend also honoured me with requests to assist him with various consulting projects, which whetted my appetite and proved rewarding. People, I discovered, still valued my expertise.

A pastor nephew enticed me to become involved in a morning program serving breakfast to some 300 street people. My expertise consisted of washing dishes, which ensured clean hands for the week but also reminded me how blessed I was.

Finally, I developed enough courage to sit down at the keyboard and translate some thoughts to writing. As I progressed, the experience, independent of quality, proved therapeutic and fulfilling. I was replacing former satisfactions with new alternatives.

Reflecting on my retirement, numerous questions come to mind and merit exploration: Why talk about it? What does it entail? How does one prepare for it? I realized that attitude and perception constitute such a vital role in every stage of life and assume special prominence in retirement. An unknown author stated, "Age is a matter of attitude, I'm retreaded not retired." William Shakespeare put it into perspective, "Things are neither good or bad but thinking makes them so."

Much is written on what makes for a full life. One unknown author summarized it well when he stated: that four things are needed to make life worthwhile: learn something new each day, do something for others each day, see something beautiful each day and laugh a little each day. This is especially applicable in retirement.

One is led to conclude that it is not so much what happens to people when they retire but what happens in people when they retire. In other words, it is the emotional-feeling component that is the prime contributor to a happy retirement (assuming finances are in place). Many people who are not used to being in touch with their feelings, experience considerable difficulty understanding what they feel. The greatest tendency is to bury such feelings, to shut them out only to be abruptly faced with the reality of such emotions when retirement is imposed upon us. This is evident in the fact that less than 25% of the population actively prepare for retirement and many of these do a superficial job of planning. Further support for this is found in research data, for the Province of Alberta, that consistently indicates some 50% of Albertans die without wills.

Concern about retirement is something which influences job performance. Industrial studies show that performance of employees often begins to decline five years prior to retirement regardless of retirement age. More in-depth studies revealed that this decrement was due largely to anxiety associated with the upcoming event of retirement. Were such concerns alleviated through insightful preparation for retirement programs, productivity would be enhanced.

Why is there so much resistance to retirement planning?

Too often retirement is seen as synonymous with growing old, being non-productive. Ours is a youth oriented society, with focus on the younger set. To be young is perceived as the ideal. This is reflected in our modern day marketing strategies. To exemplify — the new car has a beautiful blond draped over the hood snapping her artificial eyelashes. The new cool cigarette is smoked by a young macho man with lots of hair on his chest. The only ads involving older people are the kinds which refer to gum that doesn't stick to your dentures. Ads attempt to delude us into believing careful grooming, a new young wife, a dye job, a chin lift, will take 20 years off a person's age but you can't fool a flight of stairs!

I was putting moisturizer on my face when my little girl asked what I was doing. I explained that a certain cream was good for wrinkles. "It's sure doing a great job Mummy," she replied, "you're getting lots of them."

Patricia G. Ruth

Whether we like it or not the chronological clock moves on. One need only look at pictures of ourselves over a ten-year period to notice how much we have changed. People seem to react to aging in three ways: Some are very resentful. They want to live longer but don't want to grow old. I would suggest these are spoiled and immature individuals who probably never will grow up. Then there are the resigned people who are contented receiving pension cheques and watching TV, a short-lived pleasure. They need to be encouraged to get off their duff and get into the main stream of life, if it is fulfillment they are after. Finally, there are the realists who see something good and bad in the aging process but tend to stress the good side. Retirement for them is fulfilling.

> *Just once I'd like to see an article on retirement*
> *that says it's all right to sit around and enjoy it.*
> *Franklin Folger*

There are, however, more important reasons why people don't plan for their retirement: Professionals have been in control of their lives all their life and often do not want to be told by others how to run their lives; many deny the need to plan ahead. What's there to plan, they say — I can always find something to do — I'll keep busy somehow. But, keeping busy is not the problem. Feeling fulfilled, useful and creative is the ongoing, enriching, challenge for mankind. The ostrich, head in the sand, approach pays few dividends.

Retirement somehow seems to lessen the value of what we have spent our life on. It leads to such questions as: was my life worthwhile; have I really made an impact; has my presence counted? It means giving up cherished career goals which can never be accomplished. It means giving up status and recognition. For the homemaker the prospects of having a husband underfoot providing efficiency suggestions, regardless of how charming, means a loss of freedom and independence, at least during the major part of the day. Granted, it is delightful to do things jointly. However, we all need our space and opportunities for our own fulfillment. One can't achieve that on the coattails of another. Husband and wife must be in agreement on what they expect retirement life to hold for them and what they are going to do to prepare for it. The change forces couples to re-evaluate relationships — something they may not have addressed for a long time. Retirement requires as many compromises as does adjustment to marriage.

No man was ever shot in the kitchen doing dishes.
Toronto Globe and Mail

Some simply shelve concerns about retirement by engaging in untested fantasy planning. Too often such plans fail because they were not thought out or failed to address individual needs. A motivating reason for my opening a coffee shop was the erroneous belief that this would provide substitute career satisfaction. This proved not to be the case.

The worst time to work out a plan for retirement is when you retire — when you suddenly are cut off from the rewards and support systems associated with working — when one is faced with feelings of devaluation and hurts. At such a time effective planning is not possible! There are two necessary kinds of planning — financial and emotional. Financial preparation is vital but in some respects is easier. Some years prior to my retirement I spent time with my accountant working out a strategy that would meet my financial needs once I no longer held a job. Everyone must do something similar but what constitutes financial security varies markedly. It is difficult, if not impossible, to launch retirement plans without money. Nevertheless, it is important to remember that financial security in itself will not guarantee retirement contentment, but it must be addressed.

When money talks, no one worries about the grammar.
Toronto Globe and Mail

One cannot completely prepare emotionally for retirement. Certainly, it helps to be aware of the various factors that will impact on you. We, however, all come to this time in our lives with our own unique personalities, beliefs, attitudes, fears, anxieties, life experiences and expectations, which moderate how we will react. No one can experience life through another's eyes. Regardless of how well one prepares, there will be a period of adjustment and this will vary markedly from one person to the next. It is important to be prepared for this so we realize this is a stage we must all go through.

How should retirement be viewed?

I believe retirement should be viewed as another phase of living — another career — the beginning of a new life experience alive, vibrant and fulfilling, the freedom to pursue long neglected interests. I find it helpful to view life encompassing three major careers. The first career is the career of formal schooling and preparation for the world of work, which may extend from kindergarten to post secondary education. The second career is the period during which we actively pursue a career and all that entails. The third career is the career of retirement. I emphasize that this period, like the preceding, must be treated as a career if it is to be successful. This implies an active not a passive phase, a time for acquiring new and different skills, the requirement to adjust to new and different opportunities — a new vocation. This requires one to think of retirement positively. It's not a time for loafing or withdrawing. It's a chance to be your own boss to participate in life in a new way. It's an opportunity to establish your own priorities geared to self-satisfaction instead of the pay envelope — recognizing that finances cannot be ignored.

When I retired on an assured pension, I realized I actually found permanent security. My welfare was no longer dependent on what I did or what I was, on my judgement, on my reputation or on my ability, on who liked me and who didn't. No one would ever have power to fire me.

Jules Z. Willing

One must remember that one commences the career of retirement with an abundance of life experiences and a diversity of skills which haven't suddenly deserted you when you retire. The challenge is to creatively apply this reservoir of skills and knowledge in a new way in existing or new settings — unencumbered by the pressure of work schedules. Dormant interests can be tested and new attractions explored. This, however, entails experimentation. Numerous satisfactions lurk on the horizon waiting to be tasted if one is prepared to reach out. Many a famous painter didn't fully develop their talents until late in life. Just because we haven't done something before doesn't mean we shouldn't try.

On my 65th birthday I plan to move in with my parents.
The Edmonton Journal

I would suggest that part of preparing for retirement is learning to live a rounded life long before the advent of retirement — to see and take time out to smell the roses. At early staff meetings, I was often surprised how few people could recall the kind of day they encountered on the way to work. They seemed to have become so engrossed with work that they lost the zest for living life to the fullest both on and off the job. There is an old saying that is so appropriate: All work and no play makes Jack a dull boy and Jill a wealthy widow. The point is that one must get into the habit of enjoying non-work pleasures since that is what will be available when retirement becomes a reality. George Eastman puts this into perspective, "What we do during our working hours determines what we have; what we do in our leisure hours determines what we are."

We all need fulfillment at every stage of our life. If we are the kind of person who has derived great satisfaction from accomplishments, this need will continue to require fulfillment even once retired. Unless satisfied, discontent results. If the career of retirement is to be rewarding, one must develop other growing experiences. Dr A. W. Kelly, a managing editor of the Canadian Medical Association, reinforces this point when he says, "Relief from the pressures of immediate responsibilities is the first and most agreeable sensation experienced. But this will not persist for more than a few months unless one becomes immersed in a new relatively challenging occupation which keeps one's talents at comfortable stretch. During working years, a person spends a large part of everyday thinking about the job, executing it with professional competence and being pleased when it turns out well. It has become a habit of body and mind. Unproductive leisure will not take its place. An empty spoon will not satisfy a man's need for something substantial."

It is vital that one begins developing alternate need satisfiers prior to retirement and tests these in advance to ensure they yield the pay off desired.

There are numerous things one could try out in advance. I always enjoyed cooking and my wife and I collected some three hundred plus cook books, many with historical anecdotes. I discovered pleasure in trying out recipes, as long as my talented wife was out of the kitchen. Now that I have time, I can experiment to a greater degree.

I have always enjoyed wine and decided to investigate the art of wine making. This led to my trying numerous concoctions with some surprising results. I now have in excess of two hundred bottles on the shelf. My strategy is to serve my wines in fancy containers without stating the origin. If praiseworthy comments result, I modestly claim ownership.

Do not be afraid to fail. It's one sure sign of living.
Pete Zafra

With today's technology, new learning, new worlds, new experiences, are at your fingertips through the Internet. Of course one can argue that acquiring the skills needed to access this information is beyond one's capabilities. That is simply escapist talk. I think of my parents who not only had to adjust to a threatening new world, lacking the language but needed to survive, and they did. Not only that, they provided opportunities for the growth and development of their children. Their outlook made the difference. Today's retirees in no way face such adjustment challenges. If one has the will there is a way! Self-pity and whining helps little. Success in any career requires application, the acquisition of new skills and above all a positive attitude. So also, the career of retirement.

While hobbies can be satisfying, they must do more than just keep us occupied. When one is working, full-time hobbies take your mind off your work. But when there is no work it's quite different. On retirement, one doesn't need activities to take your mind off things but one needs activities that put your mind on things. Life, even in retirement cannot be completely without a goal.

> *There is no pleasure in having nothing to do;*
> *the fun is in having lots to do and not doing it.*
>
> *Mary Little*

Retirement brings with it feelings of insecurity, loss and grief. When we talk about grief the usual association is with death and dying. This is, however, an incomplete perception. We grieve for many things in our life, often forgetting that we do so and they tend to pile up. For example, we grieve: the past, moving, a home, leaving school, a familiar district and old friends — especially if they have died. We grieve our youth, the death of a dog, loved ones who have moved away, even lost hair. When we retire we grieve for the fact that we no longer have a job. The list goes on and on varying from one individual to the next. Good mental health dictates that we learn how to cope with loss and grief, accepting that it is a normal healthy process. Probably, the most difficult adjustment is the loss of a mate. One writer commented that every marriage ends in tragedy — divorce or death. As we age, all of us must prepare for this reality. Every couple must give some thought to this and consider how they would cope should they find themselves on their own — rather than waiting for this to occur when we are emotionally less equipped.

A tragedy for many widows is their lack of day to day business skills. Some left the entire management of their financial affairs to their husbands. Many don't know how to write a cheque. Consequently, when left on their own, they are devastated. Each partner should acquire such life sustaining skills in advance. Undue dependence is neither fulfilling, wise, or practical.

The significance of a supportive belief system assumes increasing importance with age. As you enter later life, you can't help but recognize that you have fewer years ahead than behind. If you have no sustaining faith the anxiety associated with aging assumes even greater prominence. Even a strong faith will not eliminate apprehension, but faith minimizes it. At this stage in my life, I would not wish to face life day to day without God's sustaining hand.

Faith is the soul riding at anchor.
Josh Billings

The importance of a support system, especially in time of grief, cannot be over emphasized. Friendships must be cultivated throughout life. As one moves about this takes considerable effort. People in new settings already have a network of friends and don't need you as much as you need them. Invariably, my wife and I found that we had to take the first step. This became increasingly so as we grew older. When we moved into one condo we invited our immediate neighbours for tea and a glass of wine. Since they liked my wine, I blessed each with a bottle which greatly helped cement relations. Now they wave to us as we go walking and keep an eye on our home when we are gone. Over the years, we discovered that people are reluctant to invade one's privacy and, consequently, stand back. Once the ice is broken, inhibitions dissipate — but it helps if one takes the first step. Friends, like flowers, must be cultivated and nurtured or the friendship soon withers. We have friends that go back forty plus years and when we get together we pick up where we left off — but we made a point of staying in touch.

Socializing is much easier when both mates are living and actively participate in entertaining. The situation changes markedly when one is suddenly alone. One might simply not have the courage, energy, or money to continue doing so. The dynamics, furthermore, for both host and guests have changed with people not knowing how to react to an altered social situation. Feeling uncomfortable, they withdraw.

A widowed friend described this well. When her husband died, friends out shopping, on meeting her commented, "How lovely to see you — let's have lunch some day." No invites to their homes however, were forthcoming. The same lady observed that, "Couples are honoured, women on their own are a pain in the neck — men on their own are a plus value to society." Nevertheless, the same socializing needs require nurturing.

Another widowed friend tells how she was told, "Inviting singles throws off the seating plan at the dinner table." Somehow, it is more difficult for women to strike up friendships than it is for men. They are looked at in a very different way.

My wife, Selma, has numerous widowed friends with whom she stays in touch, finds stimulating, and invites to our home. Those who seem to have made the best adjustment, share some common characteristics. They were not unduly dependent on their families, learned to socialize early in life, developed interests independent of their husbands, continued to grow and develop and retained a good self-image. These are all characteristics developed early in life. Nevertheless, adjusting to life on your own is challenging. Preparing for the event helps replace losses.

Often in life we are driven by the need to excel at all costs. This being so, we have little time and perhaps inclination to reach out. We devote ourselves unduly to the accomplishment of goals that reflect success. Consequently, we discover on retirement, with the world of work behind us, that we are very much alone. Worse still, we have lost the art of making friends. Samuel Johnson (1755) so eloquently described the importance of making new friends throughout life when he commented, "If a man does not make new acquaintances as he advances through life, he will soon find himself alone. A man, Sir should keep his friendships in constant repair."

A frequently neglected area is the need to ensure one's estate is in order. This means making a will. So many people refuse to address this need and, consequently, leave survivors in a terrible mess, often resulting in lengthy and costly legal battles. Without a will, the state enters the picture and distributes assets as it sees fit. I know a family who fought the distribution of a husband's estate for fifteen years to the detriment of his wife. We have a responsibility to put our house in order so that others aren't saddled with unnecessary responsibilities. My wife and I regularly update our separate wills carefully specifying who the executors are to be. There are standardized forms that can be used. We, however, have always relied on the services of our family lawyer who frequently raises issues we have overlooked. Under these circumstances, lawyers don't charge as much as people are led to believe since they are merely updating. It often is cheaper in the long run.

It is important to keep an updated file known to the executor of a will which include such information as: A listing of all assets and liabilities, the location of all bank accounts, safety deposit boxes, the location of wills including the names of executors, the names, addresses, phone numbers of accountants, lawyers, insurance and pension plan agencies as well as investment advisors. Specific instructions should be included outlining funeral and burial preferences. Care should be exercised to ensure both mates are familiar with the information on file. In summary, one should develop an action plan which will help identify the steps those left behind are to follow in processing the estate. People are emotionally distraught at this time and frequently make the wrong decisions.

Another challenge in retirement is deciding where to live. By then, in all probability, your children will have left home and you may decide that it is time to downsize. The need for considerable upgrading becomes a major motivator as well. Our family had lived in our large home for twenty-nine years. The trees we had planted had grown to an impressive size. The Mayberry tree annually provided berries for my winemaking exploits. The unobstructed view of the ravine provided peace and tranquillity. We loved our home, which was enriched by many memories.

I always said I would only leave the place feet first. In the meantime I would, if needed, get someone to do the maintenance chores. Both my wife and I were very comfortable there and to relocate carried with it the threat of destroyed memories and predictable comfort. Family changes, however, obliged us to rethink our situation. Our family of three daughters and one son gradually spread their wings. Two daughters and four grandchildren, located near by, provided much pleasure and nurturing. Our son worked in Europe and while he loved his home, would not be unduly affected if we relocated. Our third daughter, her husband and five grandchildren, however, settled on the West Coast some eleven hundred kilometres away. Consequently, we infrequently only had the opportunity to participate in their many activities. This led to a re-evaluation and a revised action plan. We decided to sell our big home, buy a condo in the area where we had lived so long and another near our third daughter and her family on the West Coast. All went well until the moving van parked in front of our home and furniture began to leave. At that point, both of us shed tears — a very emotional moment! After three years we both agree it was a good decision. We spend the summers in Edmonton enjoying the long days re-connected with our children and grandchildren. When the snow flies, we pack up and go to Langley where we become equally active in the grandchildren's many activities. While we love our children, we have no desire to live with them. They need their space and so do we.

Many on retirement say: When I retire I am going to leave the farm, I'm going to sell my house, I am going to move to the coast or some place where it is nice and hot. In many ways this is a romantic notion. While for a short time it is nice to have ongoing warm weather, beautiful climatic surroundings without friendship, without a support system, soon loses its appeal. One can always buy heat but you can't buy friendships.

Others say they plan to spend their retirement years travelling but have never travelled. The first time they do and lose their luggage, and encounter hammock-like beds, the appetite quickly weakens. Not being able to communicate in a foreign language complicates things and adds to one's feelings of insecurity. Travelling is an art that must be learned to be enjoyed and should be tested in advance.

A typical pitfall is that people make decisions without first testing the waters. It is best to rent out one's home, do a trial run in the planned location to see if it meets one's needs. Nothing is so pathetic as the people who sold their property only to discover they made a mistake and cannot return to where they left off. Too often people forget that they have spent many years developing friendships and community associations. They have an established relationship and understanding with their doctor, dentist, lawyer, etc. They know where the good buys are and are comfortable in their familiar setting where they are known and are accepted. To move away is to leave all this behind. It takes time and a great deal of effort to develop a new social network — to develop that "old shoe" feeling which comes through long associations and which becomes more difficult with age. It is best to test the water before deciding to go swimming!

In summarizing, we have found a healthy retirement must provide emotional balance and financial security. Without these, we are robbed of the opportunity to explore life-enriching retirement experiences. At the same time, we require a chance to grow and develop, a chance to satisfy well-established gratifications in varied ways. It also was very important that we had interpersonal security that comes from knowing we are wanted and needed by family and friends. Finally, we also required spiritual security that comes from knowing we have a God who loves us, cares for us and having written our names in the palm of his hand, will not forsake us.

So many people become so preoccupied with pursuing a career that they devote insufficient attention to life off the job. When they leave the world of work, it is almost like a strange re-entry into their private lives.

A man must decide while climbing the mountain what he wants
to find at the top. It's too late to start thinking about it when he
gets there. We must be able to stop spending most of our working
years reaching our career goals without ever giving a thought
to the goals we want to reach after our career ends.

Jules Willing

Chapter Twenty
What I Have Learned from
My Travels Through Life

Feelings of Inadequacy — A Human Characteristic

- None of us have immunity from feelings of inadequacy. Varying situations continue to generate such feelings throughout life. When we think the past and associated emotions have been conquered, new events trigger their recall but they dim with time. Those who insist they are not so affected are simply deceiving themselves and are not in touch with their inner self. They develop defense mechanisms that insulate them from reality. In the process, their potential is impeded by their unwillingness to constructively come to grips with such feelings.

- Often one erroneously concludes that we alone are deficient and others are not so afflicted. Believing this, we unnecessarily allow such beliefs to dominate our lives, thereby restricting development.

- Accepting the reality that all people at some time or other, under varying circumstances, are handicapped by feelings of inadequacy can yield a liberating awareness. Recognizing this can help remove self-imposed shackles that restrict aspirations. Even Einstein had limitations.

- If you don't feel somewhat inadequate, you will never identify and address the deficiencies that are there. Insight precedes growth.

- Displays of superiority invariably cloak feelings of inadequacy. Secure people have no need to hide behind such behaviour.

- Tactics, such as ridiculing others, putting others down, merely reinforces inadequacy and prevents growth and development.

- We tend to act in accordance with how we see ourselves. Others frequently see a different image. External feedback can broaden self-awareness.

- Each stage in life can be stimulating or threatening. It all depends on preparation. All require the acquisition of new skills and knowledge if insecurity is to be reduced.

- Attitudes and perceptions so often limit what we are prepared to try. It is good to be reminded that most noteworthy accomplishments are the outcomes of very ordinary people driven by the desire to succeed — often in the face of great adversity.

Dealing With The Past

- It is important to remain aware of one's past but not become encumbered by it. The past is history that has run its course. Failing to progress beyond historical happenings blurs long range aspirations.

- The past often is used as a crutch inhibiting accomplishments. Self pity, the poor me syndrome, often is used to justify inaction and suppresses striving.

- Clinging to the past is a slippery slope that clouds reality.

- It is important to move on. Nurturing past grievances and hostilities impedes contentment. Often one's hate is wasted since recipients may be long gone or oblivious to our feelings.

- Learning to forgive, even if we feel reluctant to do so, has a great liberating effect. Shaking the monkey off our back is very therapeutic. Carrying past hates and regrets greatly impedes one's walk in life.

- Adopt the Serenity Prayer, "God give us the grace to accept with serenity the things that cannot be changed, the courage to change the things that should be changed and the wisdom to distinguish one from another."

- All can reflect on events, things done or said, which generate guilt and shame wishing the slate could be wiped clean. Often this cannot be done since those affected are no longer living. Where possible, fear, pride or other reasons, should not be allowed to prevent a reconciliation. Forgiving oneself for past misdeeds often is harder than forgiving others, but it must be done if one is to be set free.

- Don't forget where you came from or look down on your heritage — build on it. Humble beginnings are not something to hide; it didn't harm Abraham Lincoln. Feeling the need to hide your origin means feelings of inadequacy still dominate you.

Be Yourself

- Discover and develop the real you. Accept yourself for who and what you are and build on it.

- Don't take on a pseudo personality that doesn't ring true and hides who you are. It only serves as a barrier to relationship development.

A Journey Through Inadequacy

- Once you start playing a role you must constantly remember the impersonation and keep playing it — a draining artificial activity.

- Learn from others, adopt their virtues but preserve the real you, the person you are.

- Avoid the trap of trying to walk in the shoes of someone you admire. Seldom do the shoes fit.

- As long as you feel the need to mimic others you haven't grown to accept yourself and likely never will.

- Discovering and developing your own abilities, not demeaning them, is the beginning of real growth and development; the key to becoming a comfortable person.

- Self-examination, not condemnation, leads to insight and reduces feelings of inadequacy.

- Find out what you are good at and enjoy. Others may help but only you can decide what generates contentment.

Growth — The Essence of Mankind

- Treat life's happenings, even though painful, as learning experiences that yield insight and mould character. The benefits will be long lasting.

- Denied the challenge of a struggle and the learning that goes with it, ill prepares one to face adversities. Life experience cannot be passed on genetically.

- A supportive, loving, but not overly protective environment helps resolve life's setbacks while developing needed life skills. One must taste sugar to know what sweet means — describing it is no substitute.

- Developing an awareness and appreciation of others feelings and needs is essential for living.

- A completely self-centred person is a maladjusted individual rejected by society and deprived of fulfillment.

- Dare to aspire — to dream. Without this, there cannot be growth. In dreaming, remember to take one step at a time. Not doing so makes the goal appear unattainable.

- Life experience that mellows a person cannot be taught — few courses help develop this skill.

- Long range vision is required for aspirations to bear fruit. Achievement is a growing process.

- Creativity must be nurtured. We all have it to varying degrees. It is never too late to develop dormant talent.

- The need for external status props, is a poor substitute for internal growth.

- Seek out the advice of an insightful and trusted friend. Good judgement is not confined to the learned few; in fact the reverse may be true.

- No one is an island unto themselves. Selective leaning on others in time of need is a normal healthy human characteristic that bears fruit.

- Ensure growth takes place off the job. One day there will be no job and prior preparation is needed to fill the void.

- Your life starts turning around when you start believing in yourself. Others can help but they can't do it for you.

Be Adventuresome — Dare to Risk

- Each new experience can be both exciting and threatening — painful or pleasurable. Doing nothing is much worse.

- One cannot shut out what is threatening by attempting to control the environment. Insulation merely reinforces feelings of inadequacy, impedes growth and inhibits fulfillment.

- It takes courage to stand up and be counted but doing so greatly boosts self-worth.

- When you no longer feel valued, move on. Don't attempt to change that which is cast in stone.

- There are times when one must take calculated risks to gain a lot. One cannot endlessly live with regrets. Better to fail than not to have tried.

- In the final analysis, every adjustment must be made by you.

- Don't be like so many threatened people who retire at thirty but die much later fearing to venture into new but promising uncharted waters.

- Undue reliance on others in decision-making, results in indecision.

Dormant Talents Yield Little Satisfaction

- Contentment flows from developing God-given gifts. It is not the kind of talent but rather what is done with it that proves satisfying. Doing little yields little rewards.

- The accomplishments of others cannot replace personal efforts. Riding on the coat tails of someone else is no substitute.

- Emulate the qualities of others but appreciate the virtue of your own uniqueness.

- Timely recognition and encouragement paves the way to success and stays with you for life.

- Don't look elsewhere for Utopia. It must be found within yourself.

- Accept success as a legitimate indicator of personal aptitude.

- Validation of our skills often requires the endorsement of a respected other.

- When little is expected of you, it is easy to surprise others with your accomplishments.

- Others may attempt to steal your achievements, but in time, the truth will out.

- There is always a gap between expectation and reality.

- An accomplishment is only what is meaningful to you.

INTERRELATIONSHIPS

- Others cannot feel your pain or your pleasures — they are your own unique experience — to expect otherwise leads to disappointment and resentment.

- Don't expect others to treat you fairly, to appreciate you for what you are. Granted, there are exceptions, but realize that man by nature is very self-centred.

- One man's discomfort is another's pleasure.

- Accept the fact that there are mean people. Don't let their hang-ups become your hang-ups.

- Reaching out and helping others markedly improves your self worth. It is the rent we pay for occupying space on this earth.

- Don't weigh things to death. If you feel like hugging someone, do so.

- Accept that certain feelings you have are justified and should not make you feel guilty.

- Criticism and ridicule levied by certain people should be viewed as a compliment.

Limitations Can Become Strengths

- All of us are flawed. No one likes a perfect person.

- Capitalize on your limitations. Terry Fox, having lost a leg through cancer, launched an on going cancer research fund-raising drive.

- Choosing to view limitations as constraints makes them so. Many a small non-threatening man has become a great therapist.

- Only a very small proportion of the population possess above average intelligence and they are not necessarily high achievers; these come from the large average intelligence sector. Passion for success and application make the difference.

- A realistic grasp of how you affect others is essential to growth and development.

- The experience gained from learning how to cope with personal deficiencies broadens one's understanding of human behaviour and helps develop relationship skills.

- Developing an awareness of limitations and balancing these against strengths, maximizes achievement.

Friendship

- Nurture your friends. If you don't, you will soon lose them especially if you move frequently.

- Friendships moderate the pain of loneliness.

- Reach out to others. Make new friends. Often you must take the first step especially if you move into a new community.

- A real friend is someone who will cry with you.

- It is not good for man to live alone. (God's advice to man)

- The older we get, the harder it is to make new friends. It is an art that must be learned and repeatedly practiced.

- Grief can take care of itself, but to get the full value of joy you must have someone to share it with.

Life is More than Work

- One day work will cease. If you have failed to prepare for that day, a void will enter your life.

- Take time out to smell the roses. Work does not replace simple pleasures.

- When you retire the nurturing derived from work ceases to exist. Alternate satisfying replacements must be developed long in advance of retirement to fill the void.

A Journey Through Inadequacy

- Few people on their deathbed regret not having spent more time at the office.

- Flowers must be nurtured if they are to mature to full bloom. So also, relationships that continue once retired.

- Don't escape from life by going to work.

- Remember we only go this way once. There are paths that lead to other places than the office.

Laughter

- Learn to laugh at yourself and the foibles of mankind. A happy disposition attracts people like honey does flies.

- Laughter often does more good than hefty doses of medication.

- Laughing at yourself is threatening to no one.

- Think back when you were a child and laughed until your sides ached. It is an experience often lost to adults yet would greatly lighten life's load.

Faith

- The poet Tennyson so aptly commented, "More things are wrought by prayer than this world dreams of."

- Harry Truman, when catapulted into the Presidency on Roosevelt's death asked the reporters to pray for him. He went on to become a great president.

- Often in life we feel cornered and defenseless not knowing where to turn. It was during moments such as this that soldiers in battle turned to God for sustenance.

- Egotistical men attempt to create the illusion of being completely in control of life. Acknowledging a need for God in one's life destroys the image of self-sufficiency.

- Man to achieve fulfillment, within the framework of his own limitations, must reach out. The search is a private one, going outside one's self. Perusal leads to contentment and peace of mind. We cannot do it on our own.

Epilogue

The completion of my book was both a high and a low point. A major goal had been achieved but no stimulating challenge was on the horizon and the threat of boredom lurked. Fortunately, before such feelings took root, I was approached by Canadian Executive Services Organization (CESO) with the offer to serve as a volunteer adviser to Holy Angel University, in the Philippines. CESO was considering several names and I was quite certain others better qualified would be chosen. To my surprise, I was selected. While flattered, I wasn't at all sure that I was up to the challenge. My anxiety increased when the University provided a titled list of those who were to participate in leadership and administration training sessions. All were department chairs or unit heads. But I dared to accept.

Twenty hours of travel saw me arriving in Manila, a completely unfamiliar culture. A night's rest was followed by a challenging ride to the University a distance of some fifty miles. It was like entering an anthill — a mixture of tricycle motor bikes, cars, and a vehicle unfamiliar to me — jeepnee, an extended passenger jeep that can stop in the middle of a street and passengers can jump on and off with fees passed to the driver through various hands. An occasional horse drawn passenger cart proceeded unconcerned amidst the traffic. Horns constantly beeped to let others know they were coming through. In the midst of all this, pedestrians wove their way in and out carrying children and holding others by hand. Mingling in this confusion were panhandlers and beggars with hands outstretched. I sat on the edge of my seat fully anticipating a crash that never came. Numerous tin roofed shacks on pilings, some under bridges, dotted the countryside. I was told that when the rains came water frequently covered entire streets in towns where there was no drainage.

Finally, after a lengthy drive, we arrived in Angeles City, the home of Holy Angel University, which was enclosed in a high wall with entry controlled by an armed guard. As we entered the University, I was startled by a very large painted banner welcoming me, the CESO adviser, for a three-week period. The banner prompted real feelings of anxiety in me. I wondered what they were expecting of me and if I could possibly live up to expectations. When the car rolled to a stop my hosts guided me past students to my room and formally bid me welcome.

Input from department heads helped me identify their areas of interest which deviated from what I had prepared, and required modification. Elaborate introductions at my first sessions, citing my credentials and accomplishments, only seemed to serve as a barrier to relationship building. When I gave a personal accounting of myself, that I was 75 years old, had four children, nine grandchildren and was somewhat intimidated by the challenge facing me and needed their help to guide me along the way, the ice was broken. The Director of Nursing helped bridge the gap when she commented that she surpassed me with eleven grandchildren. When I mentioned that my wife was a nurse she replied, "I knew there was some reason for you being appealing!" The following Sunday I was invited to attend mass, which as a non-Catholic, I felt humbled by their warm welcome.

Exchanging points of view in a culture that is extremely attuned to respecting the feelings of others, rather than focus on task completion, took considerable familiarization. Participants, however, recognized the necessity for achieving a balance and were very open to new and different strategies. As relationships of trust and respect were developed, sensitive areas were opened for examination with new and different strategies explored. I felt especially honored when numerous department heads asked for one to one consultation sessions to discuss specific problem areas. Very quickly, once relationships had been established, I found myself accepted as a member of the academic family — an intimacy I had never developed as an academic Dean in my former setting.

A high point was being invited to address some sixty Industrial Psychology students. Once again, I had spent considerable time preparing a presentation but I quickly sensed this held little student appeal. A major adjustment was required and I was unsure what to do. Student involvement is always a safe strategy but how was one to get the process started? I noted that one young man might be a willing participant. Gradually, I enticed him to come forward and he asked me, "As a psychologist, do you ever felt inadequate?" How lucky I was! Having just completed my book on inadequacy, I could speak from the heart, and students were won over. In short order, a series of personal development questions were asked such as: how do you become more confident, what steps can one take to remain committed, how can women gain greater acceptance as professionals etc. The two-hour period flew by and students wouldn't leave, requesting my card, which many wished autographed. I almost became impressed with my own importance and celebrity status. Heady stuff!

I felt especially honored to provide my perceptions of the University and what restructuring changes I would recommend. Since academic chairs had little experience in also program development and related budgeting, I was requested to make suggestions in these areas. These were well received.

The last day the University prepared a "Send-off Party" for me. Speeches were embarrassingly flattering. I had to choke back tears. I kept looking behind me to see to whom the comments were being addressed. Gifts of appreciation reflected the generous, warm and caring nature of the staff who so openly accepted me as a family member. The party ended with hugs, with one lady asking if she could pinch my cheek. When I asked for clarification, I was told it meant, "I love you and good bye." What an ending!

Early the next morning I departed for home. As I left the University, the banner was reflected in the station wagon mirror. I couldn't help comparing the emotions it evoked on my arrival with those felt as I was leaving. What a difference three weeks made!

Once again a long journey brought me home. As I left the airport in a cab a rainbow lit up the sky, a reminder to me of how rewarding life can be if one is prepared to reach out.

Postlude

Feelings of inadequacy are distressing, often come to haunt us, and are common. For me these eventually became growing experiences, which led to a better acceptance of myself.

Such helpful insights led to a shedding of self-imposed shackles and allowed for the emergence of new aspirations and accomplishments. I came out of it all a whole man richer than I would have been without experiencing feelings of inadequacy. It led me to realize that it was a worthwhile journey. This journey of discovery continues to serve as seasoning in my life as I explore new pursuits in my Third Career of retirement.

Experience also has made me aware that feelings of inadequacy and fulfillment went hand in hand throughout my life. Both were essential to my development.

ISBN 141201304-6

Made in the USA
Lexington, KY
04 May 2012